Do Carrots Make You See Better?

Do Carrots Make You See Better?

A Guide to Food and Nutrition in Early Childhood Programs

Julie Appleton   **Nadine McCrea**   **Carla Patterson**

gryphon house
Beltsville, Maryland

Published by Gryphon House, Inc. 10726 Tucker Street, Beltsville, MD, 20705 or
P.O. Box 207, Beltsville, MD 20704-0207

Visit us on the web at www.gryphonhouse.com

Disclaimer
The publisher and the authors cannot be held responsible for injury, mishap, or damages
incurred during the use of or because of the activities in this book. The authors recommend
appropriate and reasonable supervision at all times based on the age and capability of each
child.

Bulk Purchase
Gryphon House books are available at special discount when purchased in bulk for special
premiums and sales promotions as well as for fund-raising use. Special editions or book
excerpts also can be created to specification. For details, contact the Director of Sales at the
address above.

Original version
The original version of this book, published in Australia as *There's More to Food Than
Eating*, was authored by the State of Queensland (Department of Families, Youth and
Community Care).

Library of Congress Cataloging-in-Publication Data

Appleton, Julie.

   [There's more to food than eating]

   Do carrots make you see better? : a guide to food and nutrition in early childhood

programs / Julie Appleton, Nadine McCrea, Carla Patterson.

   Originally published: Castle Hill, N.S.W : Pademelon Press, 1999 under title: There s

more to food than eating.

   Includes bibliographical references and index.

   ISBN 0-87659-264-7

   1. Children--Nutrition. 2. Nutrition-Study and teaching (Early childhood 3. Food. I.

McCrea, Nadine. II. Patterson, Carla III. Title.

TX36l.C5 A67 2001

372.3 7--dc21   2001023956

Foreword

As parents, we all know that a child's early years are critical for his or her growth and development.

From time to time, we struggle to make sure our children eat healthy, fresh food because we know that the nutrition children receive during their early years is of great importance.

Research from a number of organizations has shown that young children are currently below the Recommended Dietary Allowance (RDA) in some areas of nutrition, including calcium and iron.

Tens of thousands of Queensland children consume two-thirds of their daily food intake in child care services. In order to improve nutrition levels, our government is supplying information to child care services.

The publication *Do Carrots Make You See Better?—A Guide to Food and Nutrition in Early Childhood Programs* is an excellent resource to help educate people working in child care about food and nutrition to improve the health of the children in their care.

As a parent who has relied on child care, I know how important it is to know and trust that your child is being properly cared for.

The book covers a range of information about food and nutrition activities for children, partnerships between parents and staff, and standards and policies in relation to food in child care settings.

As parents and professionals who care for children, it is vital that we fully understand the importance nutrition plays in the development of our children into happy and healthy young people.

I hope *Do Carrots Make You See Better?—A Guide to Food and Nutrition in Early Childhood Programs* will assist your organization to maintain and improve the nutrition of children in your care.

ANNA BLIGH MLA
Minister for Families, Youth and Community Care
Minister for Disability Services

There is an adage that claims we are what we eat. While it would be something of an overstatement to take this literally, like most adages, there is an important truth stated that cannot be ignored. This is particularly the case in contemporary society where an explosion has occurred in the consumption of so–called "fast food" and packaged foods with attendant questions concerning nutritional balance and longer-term dietary habits.

These matters impact upon the individual differently throughout the lifespan. As is the case in many other areas of human existence, it is the young who are most vulnerable for they are the ones with the least power and, therefore, they are highly dependent upon decisions made on their behalf by adults. Therefore, in the area of food education, adults who have responsibility for young children are as much a target as the children. In this regard, caregivers and teachers of young children in all early childhood programs are strategically placed because of their relations with both children and their parents.

Appleton, McCrea, and Patterson have undertaken an important task in producing *Do Carrots Make You See Better?—A Guide to Food and Nutrition in Early Childhood Programs*. This book not only contains important information concerning food and nutrition, but also presents the information within a pedagogical framework that can be flexibly adapted to suit a wide range of educational settings. It is this flexible adaptability that makes the book distinctive. In addition, this book has a second source of distinction from other works on the same general area—the material presented has all been field tested with teachers and caregivers through an action research project. The outcome of such field testing is the assurance that suggestions and activities contained in the manual are practical, and they actually work. And, as if this was not sufficient to ensure the integrity of the material, the authors have sought extensive peer comment and review from expert sources. Seldom are such extensive efforts made to provide quality assurance to potential users.

One final comment that must be noted is that the manual has resulted from sponsorship by the Office of Child Care of the Queensland Department of Families, Youth and Community Care. It is all too infrequent that sponsorship is provided to an area such as food education, which is presumed to rest upon self-evident principles. The decision of the Office of Child Care is a cause for congratulations as is this product that has so thoughtfully been developed by the authors.

PROFESSOR GERALD ASHBY
Former Head, School of Early Childhood
Queensland University of Technology

Contents

List of figures and tables

Figures

Tables

Preface

It has been said that the ongoing health of the people in any society depends more on food than on any other single factor. Thus, from a young age, children can learn about the importance of a varied and balanced diet and begin choosing foods for themselves. However, food can be much more than the provision of nutrition during meals. Food can be the basis of many learning experiences. *Do Carrots Make You See Better?—A Guide to Food and Nutrition in Early Childhood Programs* supports adults who are facilitating children's learning about food by using foods as the basis for many experiences.

Do Carrots Make You See Better?—A Guide to Food and Nutrition in Early Childhood Programs was funded as a research project by the Queensland Department of Families, Youth and Community Care through the Office of Child Care and was developed with extensive consultation and evaluation of the health-promoting approach used. There were two rounds of action research conducted with the full range of early childhood programs and professionals working in this area. After each round of consultation, modifications were made in line with feedback received. This resource is the product of many people's ideas and contributions.

Do Carrots Make You See Better? is a versatile book that addresses food learning and nutritional provisions in early childhood programs. It is designed to meet the needs of children and adults (both staff and parents) in child care centers, family child care schemes, preschools, kindergartens, and before and after school programs. The book contains information about how food experiences can assist children in their broad learning and development and how children learn best about food. This information can add to the professional development of staff of children's programs and the book can be used in children's programs as a source book for children's food experiences.

There are six approaches to food learning with suggestions for many hands-on food experiences. This book also offers suggestions about food provision that will be helpful for the day-to-day running of various programs.

Do Carrots Make You See Better? can be used as a reference book, as there is basic nutrition information as well as food and nutrition issues that are important for children in children's programs. There are also listings of other books and organizations that can help adults further explore food and nutrition issues. Some sections that may be particularly interesting and informative for parents are marked with a photocopy symbol. These sections may be photocopied and distributed to families. *Do Carrots Make You See Better?* will also be useful as a textbook and resource for early childhood education courses.

Within this book, the words *educators*, *early childhood educators,* and *children's programs staff* refer to all adults working with children in the following settings: child care centers, community kindergartens and preschools, family child care programs, and before and after school programs. Additionally, the contents of this book will be valuable and relevant for teachers working with children during the early years of primary school.

Do Carrots Make You See Better? is not designed to be read from cover to cover all at once. Different programs and organizations will use it in different ways. It is particularly important to state that this is a general resource book. For example, Chapter 3: Approaches to Children's Food Learning, is not meant to be prescriptive. While ideas for food experiences are given, you are encouraged to adapt them to suit the needs of your own children and their individual situations. You will be the best judge about which opportunities are suitable for the developmental age of children, and only you will know their personal and cultural interests and experiences. Learning experiences are not necessarily supposed to progress from beginning to end, but we hope you will mix and match experiences from all the different *Approach* sections.

Working with food can result in very satisfying and enjoyable experiences and we hope *Do Carrots Make You See Better?* will enhance this satisfaction and enjoyment for both adults and children.

Acknowledgments

Thank you to representatives from the following early childhood programs who piloted sections and provided feedback on the drafts of this resource during a 12-month action research process:

Birkdale South Children's Centers, Birkdale

Birralee Child Care Centre, Mackay

Bracken Ridge Child Care and Education Centre, Bracken Ridge

Bright Beginnings, West Chermside

Chatswood Hills State School Out of School Hours Care, Springwood

Child Care and Guidance Centre (Children's Garden), Morayfield

Cottes Early Childhood Centre, Townsville

Elizabeth Kindergarten and Child Care, Acacia Ridge

Family Day Care, Keperra

Ferny Grove State School Outside School Hours Care

Galbiri Child Care and Preschool Centre Inc., Townsville

Happy Day Child Care, Crestmead

Inala Community Kindergarten, Inala

Kelvin Grove Community Early Childhood Centre, Herston

Kids Kingdom, Clontarf

Kingston Community Child Care Centre, Kingston

Lady Gowrie Family Day Care Scheme, Paddington

Little Aussies Too, Boronia Heights

Montessori Educare, Underwood

Nerang Child Care Centre, Nerang

Oaklands Street Children's Centre, Alexandra Hills

Railway Kindergarten and Child Care Centre Inc., Southport

Scallywags Child Care Centre, Mossman

Smithfields Child Care Centre, Cairns

South Side Gympie Kids-R-Us-Developmental Learning Centre

St Bernard's After School Care, Upper Mt Gravatt

St John Vianney Preschool, Manly

Trinity Child Care Centre, Southport

Wonderland Child Care Centre, Hattonvale

Valuable feedback was provided by:

Meredith Parker, North-West Institute of TAFE, Burnie, Tas

Janice Sangster, Health Promotion Unit, Sutherland Hospital, NSW

Susan Ingles, Brisbane School of Distance Education

Jenny Shaw, Creche and Kindergarten Association of Queensland

The Developmental Assessment Team, Queensland Health, South Coast, Qld

Kayleen Allen, Community Nutrition Unit, DCHS, Moonah, Tas

Sharelle Rowan, The Australian Nutrition Foundation, Ashgrove

Sally Burt, Consultant, Haberfield, NSW

A special thank you to the members of the Advisory Committee for this Action Research Project for their guidance, review, and encouragement:

Liz Douglas, Secretary, Queensland Parents for Child Care

Heather Conroy, Creche and Kindergarten Association of Qld

Mike Wills, Judith Alcorn, Shelli Cornwell, Jo Searle and Sue Irvine, Qld Dept of Families, Youth and Community Care, Office of Child Care

Sandy Daniele, Australian Early Childhood Association (Qld Branch)

Hilary Marshall, Queensland Professional Child Care Centers Association

Sandra McCormick, Lady Gowrie Family Day Care Scheme

Neil Harvey, Queensland Children's Activity Network

Additionally, thank you to the following students who assisted in many ways with the research and writing of this book: Melinda Bates, Brigitte Corcoran, Tania Cramp, Annie Lam, Jessica Lui, Sarah McNaughton, Jill Moore, Beth Onus, Michelle Patterson, Louisa Smith, and Amanda Theis, with a special thank you to Roslyn Shepherd who assisted in the document development and also provided many illustrations for the original drafts.

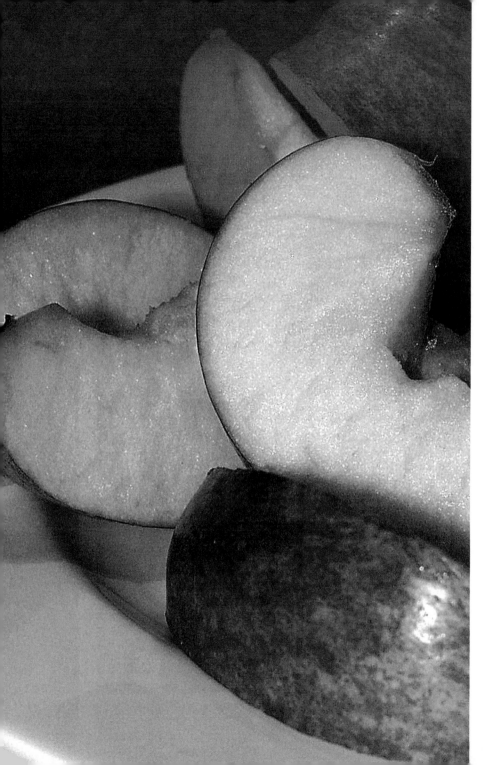

Chapter 1

An introduction to food foundations

A rationale

Food and the study of it are an important foundation for life and learning. Adults can begin to build this foundation with children from infancy and continue to construct and reinforce it throughout childhood. *Do Carrots Make You See Better?* explores what children may learn, ways that teachers teach, and how children learn. Some of the beliefs, principles, and considerations that support the overall approach or conceptual framework of this book will be developed in this chapter, and others are introduced in Chapter 2. Chapter 3 provides practical examples of developing and implementing food-related learning opportunities with children in the context of a holistic integrated curriculum. Chapter 4 outlines several major aspects of food and nutrition issues, including nutrition information, breastfeeding, introduction of solids, children with special food needs, and meal planning ideas. Chapter 5 extends the ideas found in other chapters through a self-help, self-study format with an extensive list of references.

Families and educators are encouraged to facilitate children's gradual development of understanding experiences with foods so that over time, children become autonomous decision-makers about their own health-promoting food choices.

The approach used throughout this book is to encourage adults and children to become actively involved with food ideas. It can be the beginning of lifelong development, with such outcomes as increased understanding of food issues and abilities to change one's food-related behavior. It is hoped that the ideas in this book will be used and modified, so that they best meet the needs of the children in specific settings and are comfortable concepts for both early childhood staff and parents.

Foods and food learning

The foundations for children's learning about foods encompass:
- the nutritional and health values of foods and eating;
- the roles that adults play in facilitating food events with children;
- the best ways that children can learn about foods; and
- the kinds of learning that children may gain from a wide variety of food opportunities.

Food is a vital part of our lives

Food and eating are significant aspects of the daily lives of both adults and children. Children's health and well-being are important to parents and educators; and there is increasing evidence of links between nutritional status, physical activity, and overall general health. This is true for both immediate situations and long-term health.

What we eat and with whom we eat reflect our current family and social setting. There are many examples of unique family eating, but there are also various similarities in the eating habits of families in particular communities, regions, and cultures. Research informs us (Birch, et al, 1995) that children's food-acceptance patterns are influenced by:
- *early sensory responsiveness* (newborns like sweet tastes, but not sour or bitter ones);
- *innate preferences* (by four months, infants show a beginning preference for salt, but texture and smell also contribute to flavor);
- *learning about foods* (prior experiences with foods are influential);
- *family food practices* (all infants begin with milk diets, but various solid foods may be valued and preferred or avoided); and
- *social influences* on our eating habits, such as family, peer group, the media, and advertising. For example, body image is one of

the societal messages that deeply influences food habits in our culture. From a young age, boys and girls develop views about how males and females should look in relation to strong media and advertising images. Modern society also provides a mixture of culinary temptations as well as inhibitions that influence people's eating patterns. There are many children and adults who either eat too much or too little and others who are quite confused by the conflicting messages of family, peers, the media, and society in general.

Because food and eating are important aspects of our total health (our social, emotional, cognitive, and spiritual as well as our physical health), it is important to be concerned about establishing the best food foundations for children at home, in early childhood settings, and in the broader community.

Roles of adults

The challenges for educators and parents[*] include:
- understanding how and why young children develop certain food habits;
- gaining knowledge about food variety and styles of preparation;
- being "healthful" food role models;
- being mindful of our own attitudes;
- facilitating children's gradual development of autonomous food choices (including deciding, selecting, preparing, and eating);
- encouraging habits and sharing in regular physical activities;
- ensuring children feel good about themselves; and,
- providing interesting, enjoyable, and safe food experiences.

All these challenges can be approached from a food learning perspective, where children gradually explore and understand the variety of food in their daily life through food events that are social, shared, and meaningful.

_____

[*] Throughout this book, the word "parents" is used to describe the adults with primary responsibility for caring for children.

In order to most effectively facilitate children's explorations of food, educators and parents should establish partnerships. Part of the justification for these mutually beneficial partnerships is the fact that no child, family, or children's program lives or learns in isolation. Cooperative teams may function when staff and parents work as colleagues by becoming mentors and peer coaches who:
- provide opportunities for children's food-related actions, rather than barriers;
- model and encourage healthy eating patterns;
- provide cultural and normative patterns and expectations of children's food-related events; and
- share social conventions informally during the day.

Ways of learning

Food experiences can easily incorporate a spirit of cooperation, rather than competition among children. Young children learn by doing, and this happens when reasonable choices, sustained play, and all the senses are linked. Children develop holistically, not in segments; therefore, learning opportunities that are multidisciplined and/or cross-developmental seem to best meet children's natural learning modes. The idea of providing ample time for cooperative learning via play can mean extending activities, topics, or units of work across a day or more. Rather than providing short, one-time food opportunities, we encourage you, with children, to create "bunches of grapes" that intertwine, extend, bring to life, and revisit their emerging concepts, skills, and actions surrounding foods. For infants and toddlers, as well as older children, there are benefits from adults helping them make links and build upon current and past experiences. This will happen for children when the "bunches" blend with their individual interests, their developmental experiences, and their sociocultural backgrounds. This learning scene and style might be called a learning center, a project approach (Katz and Chard, 2000), an emergent curriculum (Jones and Nimmo, 1994), a constructivist view, a scaffolding framework, or a concept-web plan. Such a balanced and developmentally sensitive offering will vary greatly for a small group of three or four infants when compared with food-oriented "bunches" for 20 children, aged three to five years, participating in teams of five or six.

Children can learn about ...

Through building solid food foundations across all of childhood, adults help children establish and strengthen their healthy lifestyle habits. Children of all ages can extend their learning in terms of attitudes, understandings, and actions by being actively involved in many kinds of food experiences. Adults teach children when they share the eating of foods, as well as when they share learning about foods through children's several areas of development and across all early childhood curriculum areas.

Children develop:

- socially and emotionally (for example, by sharing foods with others);
- physically (for example, gardening or shopping);
- cognitively and linguistically (such as discussing the process of making pancakes);
- creatively (for example, drawing or painting a picture of a potato harvest).

Children enhance their belief in themselves, their competence, and their self-efficacy when they assist in planning and preparing picture recipes. They refine their motor skills and muscle control as they use a multitude of kitchen tools—a knife, an egg beater, a peeler, a large serving spoon, and a whisk. Food opportunities tantalize all five senses, as children look and listen, smell and taste, and handle foods and culinary tools.

Additionally, children learn about the world of foods when they are exposed to foods representing a variety of ethnic communities, as well as other resources and topics from various curriculum areas. A holistic curriculum provides topics, content, and concepts for children to learn about in pairs and small groups, during the many everyday activities and events that take place in children's programs. Within educational settings, children experiment with preparing, cooking, and eating various foods. In addition, they can explore foods in many other ways, such as:

- exploring the similarities and differences of people around the world;
- welcoming visitors, such as a butcher or baker, and walking to a fruit and vegetable shop;
- relaxing with friends and food at a small round table set with colorful placemats;
- practicing social expectations surrounding foods and attending to simple safety and clean-up responsibilities;
- refining their conversational and fantasy-play language and enriching their problem-solving and factual language while talking about all aspects of everyday food events;
- advancing their awareness of the science of food and apply new science concepts about food through their five senses;
- encountering the mathematics of numbers and money, quantities and measurement, as well as spatial concepts and the passage of time by planning a grocery list, purchasing foods, or preparing an individual picture recipe;
- coordinating and constructing additional ideas about the world of food as they role play various occupations in a Dramatic Play or Housekeeping Center, or a pretend shop or make-believe restaurant;
- through storytelling and listening to the vast array of children's

Do Carrots Make You See Better?

books with topics about food in our daily lives.

Furthermore, children may explore specific concepts about foods and food cycles.

A few concepts that are of interest and relevant to most children are outlined below. Which of these concepts have you explored with the children? What other concepts about foods have you investigated? How might you introduce food sensory concepts to infants and toddlers? When might five-year-olds encounter the idea of refrigeration or spoilage?

Young children can begin to understand that:

- foods have different tastes and smells;
- foods come from various plants and animals;
- they can feed themselves;
- the textures, shapes, and flavors of foods change with processing or preparation;
- they can choose fruits and vegetables with mom and dad at a local shop;
- some foods require refrigeration;
- the amount of food needed by people depends on their ages, activity levels, and their body sizes (This is a good time to explore realistic ideas about our body images);
- some foods may or may not be eaten by their family or by their cultural group;
- we eat foods to live and grow and keep healthy;
- because foods are made up of several different nutrients, people need to eat a variety of foods to make sure they get all the nutrients they need.

A variety of children's programs

In order to identify the most appropriate food foundations for children from infancy to about 12 years of age, it is important that parents and educators consider children's general development and their individuality. Individuality encompasses family, community, and cultural backgrounds. Each early childhood setting and each program type will vary in both identified needs and expectations of children, and in potential enablers and barriers to effective food education.

This resource has been developed to support staff and parents who are living and working with children enrolled in the following educational programs: child care centers, preschools, kindergartens, family child care programs, and before and after school programs. Also, many of the standards, policies, and daily practices presented throughout this book will assist primary schools that are considering on-site eating opportunities and food learning curriculum.

It is critical that the experiences suggested in this book always be used with consideration for the health and safety of children. Early childhood educators or parents should decide the appropriateness of each experience for their particular group of children and modify or omit the experience if they are not completely confident that it can be completed safely. A safety symbol alerts readers when care is needed.

The symbol is

The food foundation needs and aims in programs will vary for children who only attend occasionally and those that are present Monday to Friday for four or five hours, up to nine or ten hours each day. There will be different food needs for infants and toddlers, such as continuing breastfeeding and the introduction of solids at about six months of age. From a young age, children are capable of being actively involved in many aspects of daily food events. Staff will be involved in menu planning for the program or providing lunch-from-home guidelines and suggestions for parents. Parents may share significant home food events with early childhood staff. Some snacks and lunches may be planned, created, and consumed by children as part of the child-centered curriculum. This approach will blend together food preparation, the eating routine, and hands-on learning as real world events shared with other children and educators. Additionally, children's food learning will be diverse and ongoing and can easily emerge from children in both approach and content. All kinds of food education can happen in early childhood settings in both formal and informal ways.

Chapter 2

A framework for learning about food

Introduction

The Food and Nutrition Curriculum Development Framework describes an approach to food education that, it is believed, will enhance children's control over their food behavior, with the ultimate aim of them engaging in health-promoting behavior related to food. The Food and Nutrition Curriculum Development Framework has been used as a basis for the food learning experiences in *Do Carrots Make You See Better?*

The Food and Nutrition Curriculum Development Framework

It is believed that if children learn about food and nutrition by practicing skills related to food, rather than just receiving information, they will eventually be able to make informed decisions about what they eat. The Food and Nutrition Curriculum Development Framework is illustrated diagrammatically in Figure 2.1. It consists of an outer layer of three key principles, which support important learning and teaching considerations, the inner layer. The central core of the framework is a decision-making learning process.

Food-related autonomy is the ultimate goal of this framework, but for young children, the journey toward this goal is just beginning. Young children do not have full autonomy in their food choices, but they should (and do) have some say in what they eat. They can begin to learn the skills necessary to choose foods that are best for their current and longer-term health and well-being.

Key principles for formal and informal curriculum

The outside layer of the framework consists of three principles that support a sensitive curriculum for children. Recognizing that children live in unique situations is essential if their needs are to be addressed.

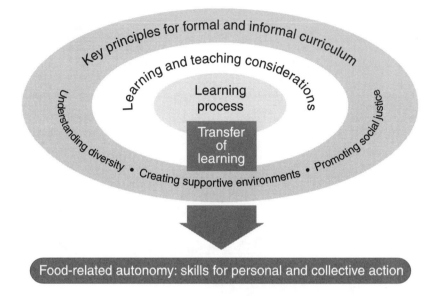

Figure 2.1 The Food and Nutrition Curriculum Development Framework

The principles of understanding diversity, promoting social justice, and creating supportive environments should form the foundation for all learning to make it more meaningful. Understanding diversity in the context of food and nutrition education involves:

▶ recognizing the contribution of social, cultural, economic, and biological factors to individual values, attitudes, and behaviors related to food;

▶ exploring different views about issues such as gender roles, physical activity, peer-group relationships, sexuality, cultural beliefs, what constitutes a healthy environment, and how this affects food habits; and

▶ exploring conflicting values, morals and ethics of considering different options and the consequences of a range of actions for well-being.

Promoting social justice involves:

▶ understanding how structures and practices affect equity with respect to food and nutrition;

▶ recognizing the disadvantages experienced by some individuals or groups (for example, remote communities or people with disabilities) and actions that can address them; and

▶ understanding how decisions about food and access to food are made at personal, family, community, and government levels, and how these affect individual, group, and community well-being.

In the context of food education, establishing supportive environments involves:

▶ recognizing the home, school (all children's programs), workplace, and community as settings for promoting healthy food habits;

▶ interaction and cooperation between the home, educational setting, and community and participation of parents and caregivers in the development of programs;

▶ sensitivity to personal and cultural beliefs in relation to making decisions about food;

▶ recognizing the crucial role that supportive physical and social environments play in enhancing food-related autonomy; and

▶ creating physical and social conditions that support children's own well-being and that of others.

These principles are appropriate for all children's programs; however, each set of staff and parents will consider how to best implement them in their setting. To some extent, the various types of children's programs will influence what happens when these principles are put into daily use.

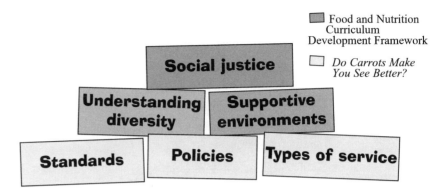

Figure 2.2 *Do Carrots Make You See Better?* links to the key principles of the Food and Nutrition Curriculum Development Framework

Also, decisions will be influenced by general and specific standards for children's programs (see Figure 2.2). Families and educators jointly consider and utilize the optional and mandatory standards that best match their particular community and program. The educational standards that you adopt for your personal approach or philosophy to food learning may include standards from an employing body or government department, one or more professional organizations, and a particular theoretical or religious orientation. Policies describe practices in a program and often incorporate the above principles and relevant standards. They may be called standard operating procedures in some workplaces. (Examples of food and nutrition policies in different programs are presented in the final chapter of this book).

Learning and teaching considerations

The second layer of the framework outlines specific learning and teaching considerations or strategies that promote the idea of making healthy food choices easier. It is important that the attitudes and actions of children's programs providers and administration staff, parents, and other community members reflect these learning and teaching considerations as they will then assist children in their food learning. Some of the important considerations are explained in Figure 2.3.

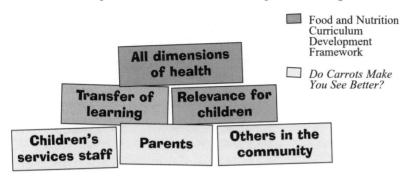

Figure 2.3 *Do Carrots Make You See Better?* links to the teaching and learning considerations of the Food and Nutrition Curriculum Development Framework

Relevance to children's needs

As children are motivated by their own desire to make sense of their world, learning needs to be relevant first to their interests, needs, and skills and second to their stages of development and previous experiences. An activity such as making sandwiches illustrates the differing competencies of children. For example, a two-year-old may participate by tearing up lettuce, while a five-year-old may grate cheese or cut the sandwiches. If learning is relevant for children, they are more likely to persist with a task, be motivated to learn more, and transfer the knowledge and/or skills to other settings (Bredekamp, 1987).

Transfer of learning

The capacity to transfer learning to other situations is essential for developing the ultimate ability of making sound food choices. Children need to feel motivated to transfer their learning to various settings. This motivation is derived from the relevance of the topic to their own world. They also need opportunities to try out newly acquired understandings and skills in a variety of settings. In the school setting, the cafeteria is an

obvious venue for practicing skills learned in the classroom. In the case of younger children, the home provides an ideal setting. Interactions between parents and children's programs staff create opportunities for sharing information about food learning in both settings (for example, helping to cook dinner, washing up, watering the garden, potting plants, and so on.).

Consideration of all dimensions of health

Health embraces physical, cognitive, emotional, social, and spiritual dimensions. It is not just the absence of disease, but is a resource for everyday living. It is important to consider all the dimensions when learning about food and food choices. Figure 2.4 details the dimensions of health and gives examples of how they can relate to different food contexts.

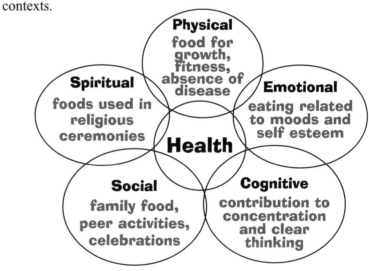

Figure 2.4 Five dimensions of health in a food context

The learning process

The learning process that makes up the center of the Food and Nutrition

Curriculum Development Framework is based on children making decisions. This is the "action" part of the framework. The empowerment-based learning process consists of a cyclical model with six skills (illustrated in Figure 2.5) that involve children (even very young children) in:

- gathering, analyzing, and evaluating information related to food, their own diets, or to societal factors that impact food beliefs or habits;
- deciding whether or not action is necessary and setting associated goals, as a result of evaluation;
- identifying barriers and enablers in relation to these goals;
- planning food actions;
- acting to achieve the goals; and
- reflecting upon what happened during food events.

All food activities should assist children in developing their competence and confidence in using these skills. Generally, the skills are enhanced by focusing experiences on one or more of the following: selecting foods, preparing foods, and advocating about foods. In Chapter 3, these focus experiences are broadened into six learning approaches for young children.

From framework to implementation

Chapter 3 demonstrates many ways of transforming the content of the Food and Nutrition Curriculum Development Framework into food foundation blocks that support food experiences for children's active involvement. If the key principles and approaches to learning are considered, there will be a standard of respect for self and others, based on valuing partnerships with conciliation and negotiation when differences arise (see Chapter 5; Sections 1 and 2). Food-related learning experiences can be integrated across the curriculum, and issues such as cultural sensitivity and concern for the natural environment can be addressed. There is a strong emphasis on democratic learning situations with many "hands-on" experiences and with children being involved in shared decision-making at every stage. The importance of play and role playing for children's learning is also acknowledged and incorporated into many of the learning opportunities.

Health-promoting practice

These theoretical concepts extend beyond providing a basis for the

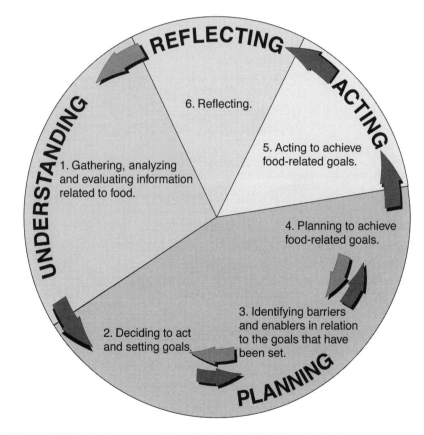

Figure 2.5 The learning process from the Food and Nutrition Curriculum Development Framework

material presented in this book and provide a health-promoting approach.

Chapter 3

Approaches to children's food learning

Introduction

Now it is time to put the food foundation blocks based on the Food and Nutrition Curriculum Development Framework into practical use. Being mindful of the ideas and concepts of the framework (the key principles, the learning and teaching considerations, and the decision-making learning process), there are many practical food learning experiences that can be implemented with young children. The idea of children constructing their own knowledge has gained strength across early childhood education. This view of children incorporates beliefs that learning can lead to development as well as result from development. It is a constructivist approach, which also encompasses the importance of social contexts, the central role of language, and the significance of adult–guided learning (Bodrova and Leong, 1995). This chapter considers children's food learning with such beliefs and approaches in mind. It is by no means meant to be prescriptive.

This chapter includes numerous suggestions for food learning experiences using six different approaches, which are discussed below.

1. Children's decision-making

Children's involvement in making decisions about food experiences should be integral to the adult and child interactions suggested throughout this book.

2. Science and mathematics

Children have naturally inquiring minds and this section may help adults and children to jointly explore some of their questions. Topics addressed include the body and the senses; science experiments; mathematical concepts; sorting and classifying; money; and space and time.

3. Food cycles

It is important that children learn where food comes from and how it is transported and transformed on its way to our plates. For example, what happens to leftovers?

4. Language, drama, and social studies

Many children's books revolve around issues and contexts of food. Books can heighten children's awareness of their own home and community and introduce them to worlds outside their own everyday experiences.

5. Physical activities and motor skills

This section suggests ways that motor skills can be practiced using food learning experiences. These skills will vary with the developmental age and abilities of individual children.

6. Food selection, preparation, and presentation

Food preparation and presentation provide multiple opportunities for children to learn and practice varied skills. Included in this book are a selection of picture recipes that, with practice, children can learn to make for themselves.

These six approaches have been developed with attention to a number of established principles of early childhood education. Significant principles include:
- children develop knowledge, understandings, and dispositions that are part of lifelong learning;
- children learn through active involvement with others in play situations;
- children actively construct meaning through multi-sensory experiences as they discover attributes and relationships;

could make something else next time. This discussion might happen during a larger group storytime for four- and five-year-olds.

However, for children aged two to three years, a small group of less than five is appropriate. It is important that children are involved in selecting and controlling these experiences.

3. Identifying barriers and enablers to making pizza

Children think about what may be a barrier to making a pizza:
- the cost of making pizzas;
- the cooking facilities are not great; or
- someone may be allergic to dairy products (such as cheese).

Ask the children to think about what will help them make a pizza:
- they have grown tomatoes in the center;
- June has herbs growing in her garden at home and could bring some in; or
- Joe's father has a pizza shop and could give them some cheese.

Help your children identify other barriers and enablers.

4. Planning to make the pizza

There are so many things to plan! For example:
- When will we make it?
- What toppings will we put on it?
- Will we make the dough with yeast, or will we use pita bread as a base? Will we make the dough one day and the pizza the next?
- What culinary tools and containers do we need?
- Who will bring in what ingredients?
- Will we shop for the ingredients and ask everyone to bring some money?
- How long will it need to cook?
- Where will we eat it?
- Will we invite some guests?

Help your children plan other steps and procedures.

5. Acting—Carrying out the plan

Prepare and eat the pizza individually or in small groups. Even older infants and toddlers can smooth out the sauce and sprinkle grated cheese on top of a pizza. Everyone in the group can share in the eating—even infants can suck on pieces of crust soaked in sauce.

6. Reflecting—Talking about and documenting the process
- How did it go?
- Who liked the pizza?
- If something went "wrong," is there some way we could make it differently?
- Will we try again?
- How else could we have gathered ingredients?
- What alternative ingredients could we try another time?
- What food will we make next time?

Other decision-making opportunities

Other decision-making opportunities could be:
- planning, preparing, and having a group picnic, a lunch for parents, or breakfast for the start of spring;
- an excursion to a Chinese, Lebanese, or Italian restaurant as part of an exploration of "Food From Around the World" or "vegetables" or any other relevant topic (for four- and five-year-olds and school-age children);
- any other excursion, such as a walk to a neighborhood fruit and vegetable shop, a bakery, or a butcher shop;
- deciding what would be a useful set-up for the Dramatic Play or Housekeeping Center, such as a coffee shop or grocery store;
- deciding on an appropriate celebration for the center as a whole or for one group of children; and
- anything relevant the children can think of.

In fact, this shared decision-making process can be undertaken with any food learning experience.

Approach 2

Science and mathematics

Introduction

Children have naturally inquiring minds. Science is a way of satisfying that curiosity in a more structured way. Most people like to experiment—to try something they have never tried before—and see what happens. Experiments are used to find answers to questions and to find ways of making new things. They are one way of getting accurate information. Scientists use several ways to find answers to their many questions. For example, they may observe growing plants or animals for a long period of time and make careful records of what happens, they may listen to different sounds, and they read what others have written about topics that interest them.

This section introduces a variety of scientific concepts including aspects of biology, chemistry, physics, and botany for adults and children to explore jointly. Some of the experiences are presented as scientific activities so children can become familiar with this type of investigation. Others are written as more flexible opportunities that can be adapted and modified to match children's needs and interests. Mathematics is a tool for making sense of the world in terms of number, quantity, space, and shape. Food activities incorporate math in a myriad of ways.

Concepts addressed in this section include:
- The body and the senses
  - The body and food
  - Body shapes and sizes
  - Teeth are important
  - The senses
- Science experiments
  - Solid/liquid/gas
  - Chemical changes
  - Experiments with plants
- Mathematical concepts
- Sorting and classifying
- Money
- Space and time

The body and the senses

The body and food

Children's bodies need food to grow and to provide energy for all the things they like to do. What happens to food in the body? How much food is needed each day? This section gives examples of some experiences that may be included as part of an exploration of this topic.

Learning experiences
- Children can draw outlines of their bodies on a larger piece of butcher paper and then draw what happens to food—mouth to stomach to small intestine and beyond. Layered puzzles are available that show the body (organs and skeleton). Children can explore some of these for ideas.
- Body aprons give a fairly realistic representation of the body organs and their position in the body. Children can try these on and "see" where their organs are. They could also use paper bags to represent their bodies, draw the organs, cut them out,

and then put them in position in the bags! Use various fabrics to create your own body apron for shared use.

▶ Children can think about what happens when they chew. They can chew a piece of food (for example, banana or bread), and feel what happens in their mouth when chewing and swallowing. They can talk about their teeth, tongue, throat, and esophagus and compare their body parts with those of other animals.

▶ Listen to each other's stomach sounds using an empty paper towel roll or a stethoscope. Discuss with children what happens when they go to the toilet and help them understand that they are eliminating leftover food.

▶ Make a stomach model! To simulate the stomach, put some food such as a banana, a slice of bread, and some orange juice into a zipper closure plastic bag. Squeeze the food until it no longer resembles the individual foods but is more liquefied. If this squashed food is then pushed through a stocking, it can represent the small intestine (some food is absorbed through the walls, but some stays inside). Show how the small intestine curls around inside the body. (We do not usually encourage wasting food, but in this case, it is an experiment to see what happens to the food in the stomach.)

▶ Save one extra meal portion from each meal eaten in the center for one day so the children can see the actual amount of food they eat in one day at the center. How much do they eat in a whole day? Add what they also eat at home. It could be explained that this is the amount of food they need in one day for growth and energy. Different people need to eat different amounts. If you run around and use up lots of energy, you may feel hungry and need to eat more food than usual. If you have had a quiet day, you may not need to eat as much, but it is important that you eat enough so you don't feel hungry.

▶ Talk with children about eating a wide variety of foods so their bodies can get what they need for growth and energy. Hygiene could also be discussed.

Body shapes and sizes

Bodies come in all shapes and sizes. Everyone is different, and we are all supposed to be different. Some people are taller, and some people are thinner. Some people have darker skin, and some people are paler. Although people may look different, there are still many things about them that are the same. They can all laugh, be your friend, talk to each other, run around, and play. Some people may not be able to do these things, but there are other things about them that are the same. For example, we all have feelings and can feel happy or sad.

Some of the following experiences could be incorporated into a learning center that is set up by the teacher. During free play, the teacher could discuss and explore the different concepts with the children.

Learning experiences

▶ Look around you. Think about other things that are the same, but different. Look at the trees outside—some are tall and thin, and some are short, bushy, and wide. They are all different. It would be a boring world if all the trees were the same! However, there are many things about trees that are the same. For example, they all have leaves or needles and trunks and bark, even though the leaves may be different shapes, some barks may be rough, and some may be smooth. Make a collage of trees, using leaves and bark. While many will be different shapes, they are all still trees.

▶ There are many types of fruits and vegetables. Cut out pictures of different fruits and sort them into similar shapes or similar colors. There are many ways you can sort the fruit pictures. They are all fruit, but they all have different shapes, colors, textures, smells, and tastes.

▶ Children (from about age two) can measure how tall they are and mark their heights on a piece of paper attached to a wall. Notice that some children are the same height while some are different heights.

- Children can draw outlines of their bodies on large pieces of paper and then paint their own lifesize self-portrait. They can put in hair, features and clothing and, finally, cut out the two-dimensional "Me." When these are displayed around the room, children can see the differences between them all. The clothes will be different, the shapes will be different, the faces will be different, but they are all still "Me!"
- Children, even those as young as infants and toddlers, can explore their bodies in front of mirrors. They can notice the similarities and differences between individuals in the group. It's OK to be different and it's OK to be the same.

Teeth are important

Teeth are important for speech development, eating, and appearance. It is important that they are well cared for. There are several factors that cause problems with teeth, including natural bacteria in the mouth, frequency of sugar intake, and infrequency of teeth cleaning. The more frequently people eat sugary foods or drinks, the more often the bacteria in the mouth are able to produce acid, which can lead to decay of the tooth enamel. Regular brushing is needed to remove bacteria and plaque from the surface of teeth.

Learning experiences

- Different animals have different teeth. What sort of teeth do your pets have? Do birds or fish have teeth? Collect jaws with teeth from various animals and compare them.
- Teeth are important for chewing and talking. Try to say "teeth" without your tongue touching your teeth.
- Chewing is good for healthy teeth. While eating lunch, count the number of times that mouthfuls of different food have to be chewed. Cut out pictures of food from magazines and sort them into those that have to be chewed and those that do not.
- Dairy foods help to make teeth and bones strong. What are dairy foods? Where do dairy foods come from? Draw pictures of dairy foods or find some pictures in magazines. Draw pictures of a dairy farm.
- Sugary foods and drinks are not good for teeth. Again, cut out pictures of foods and sort into sugary foods and those with little or no sugar.
- Soak a tooth in a covered jar of cola and record the changes daily. Put another tooth in water. Compare the differences over time.
- Children could decide to organize a "sweetless" party, with fruit, vegetables, dairy, and bread-based foods. Parents can be asked to participate in the feast! The emphasis could be on unusual, different, and attractive presentation of nutritious foods.
- Look at pictures of babies' dental development. Teeth can be cleaned as soon as they erupt. Use only a smear of toothpaste for young children as they tend to swallow it. Talk about when and how often children should clean their teeth. Rinsing the mouth and teeth with water is another way to clean your "pearly whites." A dentist or dental therapist could be invited to share models of healthy teeth with children.
- Prick a large hole in the skin of an apple and leave it for a few days in a warm, dark place. Cut in half through the original hole. Compare the skin/flesh/core to the enamel/dentine/pulp of a tooth (cross-section) and associate the rot that has spread through the apple to the way decay spreads through teeth.
- Children could role play with sugar and germs attacking teeth followed by brush and paste coming to the rescue!

The senses

The senses are particularly important for infants' and toddlers' dynamic phase of learning about themselves and their social world. (see Nailon, 1996 for a sensitive discussion of this). The five senses are sight, touch, smell, hearing, and taste. These senses help us enjoy food and also warn us when something should not be eaten. Through foods, children can explore all the senses.

Learning experiences

▶ Sight

What do fruits look like (colors, shapes, sizes)? What do vegetables look like? What about the plants they grow on? Explain different types of bread—whole and cut, inside or outside, cooked and raw.

Look at the different colors of food in the kitchen. Look for different colors in the garden (for example, red and green strawberries, or red and yellow apples).

▶ Touch

What do different foods feel like—outside and inside, and in your mouth when you eat them? Notice textures and the feel of surfaces.

▶ Smell

What do foods smell like—whole and cut, fresh and not so fresh? Do foods smell more intense when hot, at room temperature, or cold? If we can't smell foods, then the flavors are more difficult to identify. Recall when you had a cold. Ask the children to hold their noses and taste food samples.

▶ Hearing

What do foods sound like when they are eaten—something or nothing, noisy or silent, crunchy or slurpy? Listen to the sound of kitchen utensils and food being prepared or cooked.

▶ Taste

What about taste? This is one of the most important senses when it comes to food. What is the taste of raw food? Do foods taste different if they are cooked? Taste, for example, raw and cooked carrots and celery as well as raw, cooked, and dried apples and tomatoes. Hold your nose while tasting. Does it make a difference to the taste? REMEMBER: It is important to taste safe foods only—NEVER taste things that are unknown.

Other ideas: A few more sensory events to try

Set up a table where a few children can:

▶ Perform taste tests. They can taste foods that look similar in color or shape or texture (for example, salt, sugar, flour, and coconut).

▶ Taste clear liquids (for example water, lemonade, soda water, or soda).

▶ Use a "feely" box. This can be made from a shoebox, or something similar, with a hole in one or both ends where children can feel food items, but not see them. This can be used to highlight some of these senses. When the child is not able to rely on sight, the senses of touch and smell will be heightened. An opaque drawstring bag can be used in a similar manner as a "feely bag."

▶ Explore changes in foods. When food is cooked, it tastes, smells, feels, sounds, and looks different from its raw state. The concept of food changing with cooking could be explored. Also hot versus cold could be introduced.

▶ Explore raw apples with the senses and then cook some and repeat the exploration. Many things are different. Also compare raw and cooked apples with dried apples.

▶ Compare the texture (feel) of cooked carrots and pureed carrots. Do they taste the same?

▶ Explore raw pasta and then cooked pasta. It becomes soft and also increases in size because it absorbs water.

▶ Listen to sounds of food utensils, and appliances—whirring of a mixer, popping of a toaster, banging of a spoon against a bowl, scraping a plate, even hosing the garden. Toddlers can view kitchen tools while listening to them.

Science activities

For children, the world is full of new and exciting experiences and experiments. Food activities provide many opportunities for children to learn about science in everyday ways. A few examples are provided here.

Solid/liquid/gas

Introduction

Water can exist in three states—it can be a solid when it is frozen, a liquid at room temperatures, and a gas when it is heated to steam (Figure 3.2).

All matter is made up of very small invisible particles called atoms. Atoms are often grouped together to form molecules.

Solids are hard substances and the molecules vibrate gently, but do not move freely past each other. They have a shape of their own and do not have to be kept in a container.

Liquids must be kept in a container, are runny, and can be poured from one container to another. They take the shape of the container and fill the lowest part of it. The molecules move freely past each other.

In the gas state, the molecules move very fast and escape from each other. They can spread out to fill a larger space.

Water can be found in these three different forms and can be changed from one to another easily.

Figure 3.2 Water in three states

Experiment 1: Liquid to solid

Purpose: To explore liquids freezing into solids.

Materials: water

ice tray

plastic bottle (for example, a soda bottle or small drink bottle)

funnel

freezer

Procedure: Children can pour water into the ice tray and put it in the freezer.

and/or

Make a mark on the edge of the bottle and fill the water up to it using a funnel. Put a lid on it loosely and put it in the freezer.

Observe: When frozen, ice cubes can be inspected. They are now hard and do not have to be kept in a container (as long as they are kept very cold). They are solid. However, what happens when they are left in a saucer at room temperature?

Look at the ice in the bottle. Is it now higher than the mark that was made before freezing. Allow it to defrost and see where the water level is now. Water is unusual because it expands when it is frozen, while most other substances contract.

As the ice melts, notice that it always stays on top of the water. Ice always floats because it is less dense than water.

(Water is liquid at room temperature, but other substances are solid and turn to liquid when they are heated. Melt chocolate, butter, and so on.)

What about food?

1. Fruit is mostly water, so many fruits freeze beautifully. They are just what is needed on a hot summer day, but children seem to like juice ice cubes anytime.

Children can experiment with different types of fruit and vegetables and see what happens when they freeze them. Try peeled and quartered oranges, watermelon cubes or balls, peeled and sliced bananas, whole grapes, and pieces of pineapple. Eat them while they are still frozen. Try them as an alternative morning snack.

2. Fruit and vegetable juices can be frozen in ice cube trays. Children could squeeze oranges to make the juice or use commercial fruit juice. Try tomato juice ice cubes. If a juicer is available, other foods such as apples or carrots could be juiced. Place them in the freezer for about 30 minutes until partly frozen, and then insert a wooden stick into each cube and freeze. A little hot water on the bottom of the tray will help when removing the blocks.

Figure 3.3 Experiment 1

Experiment 2: Liquid to a gas

Purpose: To explore liquid turning to a gas.

 TAKE CARE This is a potentially dangerous experiment and should only be done with adults and a small number of older children working together.

Materials: water

electric kettle to boil water

china plate

saucepan on a hot plate

Procedure: Children can pour water into the kettle. Be sure the cord is away from the edge of the table. Turn on to boil.

and/or

Boil water in a saucepan. Put a mark on the saucepan at the level of the water.

and

When steam is coming out of the kettle or saucepan, the teacher can hold a cool china plate in the steam.

TAKE CARE *Be careful; use gloves or mittens and talk about safety and dangers.*

Observe: When the kettle boils, steamy clouds come out of the spout. This is steam water that has been changed into a gas. It has no shape.

When the water in the saucepan has been boiling for some time, check where the water level is compared to the mark. The water that is lost has been converted into steam.

If a cool plate is held over the steam, water will form and begin to drip back into the saucepan.

TAKE CARE *The teacher should hold the plate, with an oven mit, to avoid any scalds by the hot steam.*

Figure 3.4 Experiment 2

What about food?

1. Steaming is a great way to cook vegetables. Children could select vegetables (for example, carrots, beans, peas, potatoes, pumpkin, celery, or zucchini). They can be washed, peeled if necessary, sliced, or chopped. Boil a small amount of water in the saucepan. Place prepared vegetables in a steamer, place over the boiling water, cover with a lid and cook until just tender. Try to find a clear Pyrex saucepan, so the vegetables that are cooking and the steam can be seen.

2. Popcorn is special corn that has a drop of water in each kernel. As the corn is heated, the water is turned to steam, which expands, breaks the hard kernel, and out pops popcorn!

Flying popcorn (for children over 3 years) or noisy popcorn (for younger children)

 Use only with older children and decide if this is a safe and suitable experience for the group. Be sure children stay seated while corn is popping and do not reach for the hot popcorn.

Materials: a clean queen or king size bed sheet
electric frying pan
2 tablespoons of canola or sunflower oil
½ cup popcorn

Procedure: This should only be done with a small group of children. Everyone should wash their hands before beginning. Spread a large bed sheet on the floor, and talk with the children about sitting around its edge and not moving until all the popping stops.

Heat oil in the pan with the lid on. Test heat by adding one kernel; when the kernel pops, the temperature is right. Add the rest of the popcorn. Cook without the lid. Popcorn will "fly" out of the pan. When it has finished popping, the corn can be collected. YUM!

Alternatively, for noisy popcorn, pop the corn with the lid on and children can listen for the popping. First there are few pops, then lots, and then few again. Talk about why this happens.

 Keep the hot pan out of the reach of children.

Experiment 3:
Solutions—dissolving and evaporating

Purpose: To explore solids dissolving in liquid and then becoming solid again. What does water do to sugar, salt, and sand? Does sugar dissolve faster in hot or cold water? What happens to the sugar when water evaporates?

Materials: water
clear, strong glasses or plastic containers
salt
sugar
sand
large-handed timer with seconds
saucer

Procedure: Children can put a tablespoon of sugar in a glass of water and stir. Do the same with salt and sand in separate cups.

Observe: The sugar and salt both dissolve in water after some stirring, but the sand does not.

Procedure: Using glasses of the same size, put cold water into one glass and the same amount of hot water in the other (be sure the glass is able to withstand the heat). Put one tablespoon of sugar in the hot water, stir gently, and see how long it takes for it to dissolve. Now put the same amount of sugar in the cold water, stir gently, and see how long it takes to dissolve. Count the seconds it takes to dissolve.

Observe: The sugar dissolved faster in the hot water because the molecules of water are moving faster in the hot water.

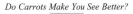

Procedure: Half-fill a glass with hot water. Stir 3 tablespoons of sugar into the water. Now place 2 tablespoons of the sugar solution in a saucer and let it stand.

Observe: After the water has evaporated, what is left in the saucer? You will find sugar in the saucer. The water evaporated, but the sugar did not.

What about food?

Children could make individual servings of gelatin. These look great in clear plastic disposable glasses. Put a slice of fresh or canned fruit in the bottom first. For older infants and young toddlers, gelatin can be prepared with the liquid reduced by $1/3$ to $1/2$. This results in a very rubbery finger food that when set can be cut into cubes. Instead of using commercial flavored gelatin crystals, plain gelatin can be used to turn fruit or vegetable juices into gelatin.

Chemical changes. Why are things different when they are cooked?

Introduction

Many foods change when they are heated (cooked). This may just be a physical change, such as melting or dissolving as discussed in the previous section or it may be a chemical change. Some foods get softer (spaghetti, vegetables); some foods get harder (eggs, dough).

Experiment with these food changes. Encourage children to guess and predict what will happen.

Experiment 4: Why is toast brown?

Purpose: To explore what happens if bread is heated.

Materials: bread (maybe a selection of different types)
toaster
optional: grill

TAKE CARE Beware of hot surfaces when children are involved in this experiment.

Procedure: Put bread in a toaster for different times (various settings).
or
Cook some bread in the toaster and some under the grill. (Strict supervision is required!)

Observe: If the toaster is on LOW the toast may become harder but not turn brown. With a little longer exposure to the heat, the toast will be just right, but if it is turned up too high, the toast will be blackened. First, heat made by the toaster dries out the water on the surface of the bread and causes it to form a dry, crisp crust. The brown color develops as the sugars and starches in the bread undergo chemical change. If the toast is heated for too long, it will burn.

If the bread is toasted by different methods, it will have different textures. This is because the amount of drying is variable.

Record: Children may document the changes to the bread by creating a collage with torn pieces of white, beige, brown, and black paper.

Experiment 5: What is baking powder?

Purpose: To discover the properties of baking powder.

Materials: baking powder
water (room temperature)
vinegar
clear glasses

Procedure: Mix baking powder into a glass of water.

Also mix baking powder and vinegar in a glass. A little food coloring can be added for interesting results!

Observe: Bubbles and froth are formed. Baking powder contains baking soda (base) and acid. In the presence of heat or moisture, the base reacts with the acid to produce carbon dioxide (CO_2) bubbles, the same as those you see in soft drinks. Vinegar is acetic acid, so this will also react with the base in baking powder to form bubbles.

An example from one early childhood program: In one center, the production of bubbles led to the construction of frothing, colorful volcanoes, which in turn led to a discussion of erosion!

What about food?

Baking powder is used in most baking recipes that do not rely on yeast for rising. The bubbles swell the food being baked, resulting in, for example, muffins that rise. Pancakes, banana bread, scones, and biscuits all use baking powder, which causes them to rise rapidly in a hot oven. They are fun to make and good to eat.

Figure 3.5 Experiment 5

Experiment 6: The use of yeast

Purpose: To decide what yeast needs to become active.

Materials: dry yeast
3 clear glasses
warm water
sugar

Procedure: Put a teaspoon of yeast in each glass. Leave one glass dry. Add warm water to the second glass until the glass is half full. To the third glass, add warm water and one teaspoon of sugar.
Set all three glasses aside in a warm place for about half an hour.

Observe: Nothing will have happened in the dry yeast glass or the yeast and water glass. In the glass with water, yeast, and sugar, there is plenty of action! There are many bubbles. These are bubbles of carbon dioxide (CO_2). Yeast is a single cell non-green plant (fungus) that feeds on sugar and releases carbon dioxide gas.

What about food?

In bread, the yeast also feeds on sugar to produce carbon dioxide (CO_2). It is this carbon dioxide gas that makes bread rise. When the dough is cooked, the trapped gas leaves the little holes you see in bread that give it its appearance and texture. Try cooking bread or a crust for pizza using yeast.

Experiments with plants

Introduction

Plants (especially weeds!) seem to grow everywhere. Have you ever looked closely at what happens when a plant begins to grow? Have you shared these natural events with children?

Figure 3.6 Experiment 6

Experiment 7: Observing plants sprouting

Purpose: To examine influences on seeds growing into plants.

Materials: clear plastic jars with lids (for a group or individual)
garden pots
seeds—perhaps a variety (bean, radish, corn)
sandy soil or moist paper towels

Procedure: Fill the jars with the soil and moisten, but do not over-water as there is no drainage in the jar. Pack the soil fairly tightly and make it level with the top of the jar. Plant seeds close to the side of the jar so they are visible. Place the jars without lids in a warm, light position and examine them every day. If the soil becomes dry, add a little more water.

Observe: The roots and then the shoots will sprout from the seeds. Do the different types of shoots look the same? Draw them, measure them, and record their growth.

Procedure: Before the sprouts break through the surface of the soil, put the lid on the jar and turn it upside down. Be sure that the soil is not disturbed and leave it upside down for a few days.

Observe: The root and shoot will both turn around and begin to grow in the other direction. There is something in the plants that causes the tops to grow towards the light and the roots to grow in the direction from which gravity pulls.

The plants will not survive for long in this environment. It may be possible to plant them into pots or a vegetable garden and then watch them flower and produce fruit. Note: Instead of using soil in the jars, moist paper towels can be crumpled up and large bean seeds sprouted in them.

Procedure: Plant seeds in at least two similar pots. When the sprouts have emerged, put one pot in a light place (for example, outside or on a windowsill), and the other in a dark place. Leave them like this for about a week, and then allow some light to reach the one in the dark and move the pot in the light to a darker place.

Observe: After a short time, the plants will look different. The plant in the dark will be paler and probably more lanky than the one grown in more intense light. When the pots are moved into reduced light conditions, they will grow towards the light.

Talk about and record: Children could discuss and draw pictures of what happens to the seeds and young plants.

Figure 3.7 Experiment 7

What about food?

The children can create an alfalfa farm. This enables the children to observe the complete process of seed growth into a healthy food in just a few days.

Day 1

Soak $1/4$ teaspoon of alfalfa seeds overnight in a small, clear jar of warm water.

Day 2

Drain. Cover the top with cheese cloth (or an old stocking) secured with a rubber band.

Days 2, 3, 4

Put the jar on its side in an open paper bag, or cover it with a paper towel. Rinse three times a day. Drain well each time.

Day 4

Put the jar in the sun to develop chlorophyll (the green color).

Day 5

Store in a covered container in the refrigerator.

Serve with peanut butter, cheese, or lettuce on a sandwich or eat straight from the jar!

Select other edible seeds to sprout and eat.

Experiment 8: To show the movement of water up the leaves of a plant

Purpose: To observe that water moves up the stem of a plant.

Materials: 2 glasses about 4-5 inches high
2 different food colorings (such as red and blue)
stick of celery, about 8-9 inches long

Procedure: Fill the glasses $3/4$ full with water and color one blue and the other red. Put the glasses side by side. Cut a slit in the stick of celery half way from the bottom. Put one side of the celery stick in one glass of colored water and the other side in the second glass. Let this stand for about two hours.

Observe: Notice what has happened to the color of the celery. The red will have gone up one side and the blue the other. Ask the children to speculate how this could happen.

Procedure: Take the celery stick out of the water and dry it. Cut across the celery stick.

Observe: You will see spots of color that show where the colored water went up the stem. These are the water tubes of the stem. Water goes up the stem through these tubes. Use a magnifying glass or hand lens to see the color droplets in greater detail.

Record: Some children might be interested in recording this process by painting or drawing. Older children may like to record what is happening using illustrations and diagrams. Adults may write younger children's words.

What about food?

How many foods do we eat that are stems and leaves? Examples are celery, lettuce, Swiss chard, and cabbage. Children could make celery boats: cut slices of celery about 1-2 inches long. Fill with peanut butter or cottage cheese. Decorate with raisins. Make lettuce rolls filled with cheese, grated carrot, steamed rice, or all three together!

Experiment 9: The growth of molds

Purpose: To determine what is the best environment for growing molds.

Materials: 4 cereal bowls
2 slices of bread
plastic wrap

Procedure: Place half a slice of fresh bread in each bowl. Cover two of the bowls with plastic wrap. Put two of the bowls, one with wrap and one without, in a warm, dark place. Put the other two dishes in a cold place, such as the refrigerator. After about three days, look at the pieces of bread. If there is no mold, put it back and wait for another day or so. This could also be tried with cheese and orange skins. Compare the different molds that form.

Observe: See whether there is any mold on any of the slices of bread. If mold appears, it will most likely be on the bread that was covered by wrap and stored in a warm, dark place. Mold or mildew grows best where there is not much fresh air, where it is warm and dark.

What about food?

Some molds spoil foods. How would you stop molds growing on food such as bread and cheese? It is best to keep them cool. However, some molds can be eaten. Perhaps children could talk about and taste mold on camembert or blue cheese.

Mathematical concepts

There are numerous ways that math can be incorporated into food experiences. Here are just a few suggestions.

Learning experiences

Counting/grouping

Children could start with a picture recipe (for example, a recipe for fruit salad or fruit kebabs). They could count the number of different types of fruit, count the fruit of similar color or shape, and count the number of pieces into which they are cut. The possibilities for counting are endless!

Group the pieces of fruit in threes or fours. Count and group the foods in *The Very Hungry Caterpillar* story.

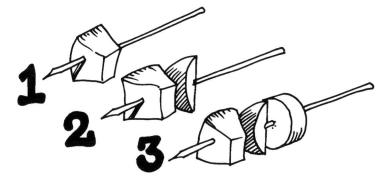

Figure 3.8 Using food in math learning

Mathematical manipulations

If the recipe is for two people, how much of the ingredients will be needed for four, or for one? For example:

- sharing—dividing in half;
- fractions—dividing potatoes into two, and then dividing these halves in two to form quarters and so on until you have potato chips;
- adding—"one more makes five";
- subtracting and the concept of zero; and
- one-to-one correspondence—one place mat for each chair at the table equals one setting for each person at morning snack.

Measuring

Using several containers of different shapes, guess which one holds the most. Fill them with water and pour each into the same size containers to check the result.

Recipes are great for the development of practical measuring skills. There are many opportunities for measuring. For example, half a cup, 1 tablespoon, 10 cups, 2 teaspoons, a pinch! Use individual recipes so each child can practice using a variety of measures.

Measure spoons of different sizes. Which spoon is the biggest and which is the smallest? Arrange utensils in order by size. Provide measuring spoons and cups for the home corner, the water tray, and the sand box.

Plant runner beans in the garden or a pot. Measure the growth of the plant and then the beans each week. The growth could be recorded on a graph. Count the number of beans. Sort them into short/long/middle.

Measure each other's heights. Some people are tall and others are smaller. Repeat later in the year. Some children will have grown more than others.

Weighing

Hold different containers and estimate which is the lightest. Weigh them on scales and see if you are right.

Weigh different fruits and vegetables, such as an apple, a grape, and a bean. Guess how heavy they are.

In containers of the same size, put sugar, cereal, and noodles. Order them from heaviest to lightest. Then add to the lighter substances until they are all the same weight. The same volume does not always mean the same weight and the same weight does not always mean the same volume.

One-quarter cup of unwhipped cream is a different weight than $^1/_4$ cup of whipped cream. Compare weight on scales.

Experiment in water with objects that float and sink. Lighter objects will float and heavier (denser) ones will sink.

Quantities

Explore various amounts of foods and liquids—more, less, the same amount.

Look at an amount of food to be stored and decide which size container to use.

What size bowl will we need to beat an egg and which one will we need to mix 3 cups of flour and some sugar?

Working from children's interests and relevant everyday events, design additional learning opportunities and incorporate other concepts linked with quantities.

Sorting and classifying

Different things are called different names. Some things can be grouped. There are many different ways of grouping things. Examples are:

- things that are food and things that are not;
- types of food—fruit, bread, meat;
- the way food is processed—canned, frozen, dried;
- color, shape, texture of food;
- cooked and uncooked food;
- food that is eaten hot and food that is eaten cold;
- food that has to be kept in the refrigerator and food that is kept on the shelf; and
- plant and animal sources of food.

Learning experiences

Children can be involved when putting away groceries by sorting the food into where it is stored. They can also put utensils away after washing up (for example, dinner knives in one drawer, forks in another).

Sorting game: Children could cut food-related items from magazines. On a large piece of paper, glue a few pictures of different types of items related to food. Examples could be a fruit, a can of tomatoes, broccoli, a refrigerator, and a farm. Children could then use the remainder of the pictures to match in some way with the pictures on the paper. There are no incorrect answers. Every answer is acceptable. See how many different types of groupings can be devised.

Make a food collage and food puzzles. Put together pictures of food cut from advertising brochures and magazines into a group collage of:

- breakfast foods;
- cold foods;
- red foods; and
- grains and cereals.

Older children can cut out food pictures, paste them on heavy cardboard, and then make personal puzzles by cutting the cardboard into random shapes.

Money

Money is of interest to children at a very early age. Children can learn mathematical skills as well as social skills, such as negotiation and sharing, when "trading" or playing with money. Play and real money can be used, as well as money from several countries.

Learning experiences

Counting, adding, and subtracting money.

Talk about relative costs when putting away the groceries—inexpensive, "on sale," or expensive.

Children could set up a shop and "sell" the produce. They could make their own money—designing (drawing or painting and cutting out) paper money and covering discs with aluminium foil to make coins.

Children could make a poster of different fruits and vegetables (drawings or magazine pictures) and leave spaces to write the prices of the items. If this were laminated, the prices could be written in felt pen and then changed as the "price" of the groceries became less or more expensive.

Make an automatic teller machine so children can "get money" and then buy from the shop.

Grow herbs in the garden and sell them to families.

What about food?

Older children could be involved in buying ingredients for a recipe (for example, a dip and vegetables). They may be able to work out what money was needed for each item and go on a shopping excursion to buy ingredients. Then, they could prepare the dip and eat it with the vegetables.

Space and time

The concepts of space and time can be very abstract and difficult for young children. Many of the experiences suggested here have been included in other sections of this book, but the concepts of space and time may not have been highlighted.

Learning experiences

The concepts of large and small

Watching and measuring dough expand—growing from smaller to larger.

Watch sprouts grow—this takes longer, but the growth could be charted each day.

Illustrate that some fruits (packages, cans) are large, and some are small. A child can eat all of a small can of fruit, but it may take a whole family to eat the contents of a large can.

A lot of water (for example, in a jug), will not fit into a small container such as a glass.

Inside and outside

Look at the inside of a fruit and compare with the outside. Interesting examples may include pineapple, pear, banana, coconut, kiwi, peas in a pod, and the "star" when an apple is cut crosswise.

Skin is on the outside of a person but a stomach is on the inside. Sometimes you cannot see the inside. Find a book with pictures of what we look like on the inside.

Near and far

Children can collect the dishes or bowls near them and take them further away.

One child can sit near the door for afternoon snack and another can sit farther from the door.

Make up a game about near and far.

Time

For younger children:
- breakfast time;
- time to clean teeth;

- time to wash our hands;
- time to prepare for lunch; and
- time to go home.

For older children:
- sequence of times to eat—breakfast in the morning, lunch at __? and dinner in the evening;
- time taken to poach an egg (use a sand timer); and
- we have snack at __? o'clock.

Ordinal concepts

First, second, third, and so on. Recipes are ideal for this. Which ingredient goes into the bowl first, which is second, and which is last?

Discuss the concept of time and duration. We clean our teeth *before* we leave home in the morning and *before* we go to bed at night. We eat lunch *after* we play and *before* we rest. We wash hands *after* going to the bathroom and *before* doing any food experiences.

Choose a recipe where things have to be cooked (processed) for different amounts of time. First mix the ingredients inside the bowl for a *short* time, and then pour the mixture into an oven dish and cook in the oven for a *long* time.

The first meal of the day is breakfast, the second is lunch, and the third is dinner. In between, we eat snack.

Approach 3

Food cycles

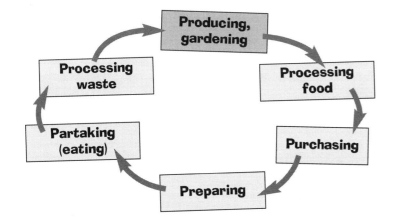

Figure 3.9 Six steps in a food cycle

This series of experiences has been created for children to learn about food cycles. The food experiences include where food comes from, how food is processed and prepared, and also what can be done with leftovers (McCrea, 1996). Children think about the processes and can learn that food does not magically appear on their plate. "The experiences we provide help to plant the seeds of curiosity, interest, understanding and caring in children" (Berman and Fromer, 1991). Examples of food cycles that children could explore are the production of honey, the growth and ripening of a tomato, where milk (cream, butter) comes from, and from wheat on the farm to bread on the table.

Producing

> **IDEAS FOR PRODUCING EXPERIENCES**
> > Deciding what to produce. Why?
> > Preparation of the ground, pot, or other container.
> > Planting of seeds or plants.
> > lettuce, tomato, corn, strawberries, potatoes, sprouts, and herbs.

Producing foods includes, for example, children's involvement in sprouting mung beans or alfalfa seeds, growing herbs in containers, or vegetables and flowers in a garden bed. Children can also plant "leftovers" (for example, avocado, tomato, or cucumber seeds, potato and sweet potato eyes, or pineapple tops). The related tools and containers are important learning tools.

It is beneficial if gardening experiences are linked to other curriculum areas in the center. An interest in gardening could begin with a story book or a discussion about a visit to a farm. Gardening experiences can be provided on an ongoing basis (digging, watering, potting, planting, picking, pruning, and so on).

Children can learn about and care for animals. Chickens are great pets for families and early childhood programs. They produce eggs that are ingredients in many dishes. Explore other food-producing animals and by-products that children can have direct contact with. Hatching eggs and raising day-old chicks will fascinate all ages from infancy.

Where to begin?

Even if you are not ready to plant the plants, there are many things that can be done in preparation. For example:
- building worm farms;
- collecting and recycling organic material into compost;

- collecting and constructing seed trays (egg cartons) and pots;
- collecting seeds; and
- germinating seeds and examining growth needs (see page 42).

Where to grow?

The first task to be undertaken if planning to produce foods is to decide where this will happen. There are many possibilities including:

- a garden—children can dig and prepare the soil;
- a no-dig garden—layers of newspaper, straw, compost, more straw and soil, built up on top of existing soil surface;
- in pots—recycled tin cans or cut-off milk cartons with drainage holes can be used;
- in a garden away from the center—if there is no room at the center. Someone from the community close by may be willing to allow the center to use an area of their garden (offering to share the produce with them may be an added incentive!);
- a person living near the center may have a vegetable garden and be happy for children to visit several times during the year; and
- sprouts can be grown quickly, indoors in clear containers.

In hot climates, it is best to grow vegetables in the summer.

How long will it take?

The following time-frame will give you some idea of how much time is needed for growing many vegetables with reasonably short growth cycles. Some will mature more quickly. (Knight, 1993):

Week 1

Garden bed preparation, and tool use and safety.

Week 2

Variety selection and garden design (create a plan).

Week 3

Planting slower growing vegetables.

Week 4

Mulching.

Week 5–6

Maintenance, natural pest and weed control, and fertilizing.

Week 7

Planting faster growing vegetables.

Week 8–9

Mulching, maintenance, natural pest and weed control, and fertilizing.

Week 10–14

Maintenance—pest and weed control.

Week 15–18

Harvesting—preparing and consuming.

Processing

EXPERIENCES FOR PROCESSING
> Why process foods?
> Make tomato sauce/jam/peanut butter.
> Make butter/yogurt.
> Visit a factory (for example, a cannery).
> Freeze fruit.
> Drying foods.

The processing of food is usually carried out to preserve and keep it. Processing food is an example of using natural resources now, but being able to eat them later. Some ways of processing food are drying, smoking, cold storage and freezing, pickling or salting, boiling and canning.

It is often difficult for children to understand that a processed food product came from a particular source and may have originally been very different in many ways. Processing activities raise awareness of changes in foods, particularly sensory differences such as taste, color, smell, and texture. The processing of food can be observed within the community and children can participate in the processing of these same foods at the early childhood program or at home.

Examples are:
- ◗ making butter—add herbs, garlic, tomato, or orange— use the buttermilk, which is the liquid formed when cream is beaten, to make scones and then spread butter on the scones;
- ◗ making peanut butter;
- ◗ drying apple or tomato slices or apricot halves; and
- ◗ making jam, tomato sauce, or pickles.

And for the younger children:
- ◗ mashing pumpkin or banana; and
- ◗ making milkshakes (milk, yogurt, grape juice).

Recipes for processing foods

1. Individual recipe for Peanut Butter (a single serving)

Ingredients
10 unshelled roasted peanuts. (These can be shelled by the children.)
$^1/_2$ tablespoon olive oil

Method
Grind shelled peanuts finely in a meat grinder or food processor, or use a mortar and pestle.
Add olive oil and mix into a paste.
Use as a spread on bread and crackers or spread on celery sticks or apple slices.

2. Group recipe for Tomato Sauce

Ingredients
1$^1/_3$ fresh ripe tomatoes
1 onion
salt, pepper
mixed herbs, paprika
1$^1/_2$ tablespoons brown sugar
2 tablespoons vinegar

Utensils
chopping knife
sieve
saucepan

Method
Wash and chop tomatoes.
Chop the onion finely.
Cook tomatoes and onion in a frying pan until very soft.
Mash the tomato and onion and press through a sieve into a saucepan.
Simmer for 30 minutes.
Add salt and pepper, herbs, paprika, brown sugar, and vinegar.
Stir and cook slowly for an additional 15 minutes until very thick. Refrigerate until needed.
Use as a dip with corn chips or raw vegetable pieces.

3. Drying apples

Ingredients
2-3 apples
fresh lemon juice

Utensils
peeler or paring knife
plastic needle with large hole
string

Method
Peel apples and remove the core.
Slice apples into chip size circles, not too thin.
Dip the circles in lemon juice.
Thread string through the apple slices one at a time.
(Don't let the apple slices touch each other.)
Hang the apple slices in an out-of-the-way, dry, airy spot by attaching both ends of the string to something sturdy.
Turn the apples every day and try to be patient! It takes about seven days.
As an alternative (especially in summer or a humid climate), hang the circles in a very low temperature oven with the door open.
Eat apples when removed from the string or store chips in a paper bag until you want them.

Purchasing

QUESTIONS AND IDEAS FOR FOOD PURCHASING EXPERIENCES
> Where do we purchase food?
> How much money do we need?
> Buy seeds to grow.
> What are we buying? Make lists.
> Buy food for recipe. Look for little packaging.
> Comparison of costs. Be a wise consumer.

Planning meals and menus or developing a gardening experience is a decision-making process that precedes shopping excursions. Young children can be involved in such planning if teachers gradually encourage understanding of food items, ingredients, and recipes. Purchasing can be a real shopping experience, or children could set up the Housekeeping Center as a shopping center and be encouraged to sort, classify, and store items in different places. Children can make their own money using buttons, silver paper, different colored paper, or whatever else they want.

Purchasing food can also involve children in writing lists, making mathematical manipulations with money, and comparing costs. Issues such as being a wise consumer by purchasing foods on "special" and fruit and vegetables in season can be addressed as well as environmental issues such as buying items with little or no packaging.

See page 46 for learning experiences related to money.

Preparing

FOOD PREPARATION THINKING AND ACTING
> What are we preparing? For whom?
> Gather utensils. Wash hands.
> Make something simple or complex.
> Make individual or group recipes.
> Drinks and containers.
> Wash up, clean up, tidy up.

In small groups, children can be involved in food preparations every day. Preparing food includes working with raw and cooked ingredients. Children can be involved in cutting fruit for a fruit salad, or spreading avocado on whole wheat toast, or hand-juicing orange halves for an individual fresh orange juice. Preparing muffins, pancakes, and fried rice all require the development of numerous skills. During ongoing food preparation, there should be a focus on awareness of a varied and balanced diet. The social potential of food tastings and meals is important, too. Therefore, provide a variety of food combinations and cultural styles. Culinary utensils and equipment and the scientific processes of cooking, safety, and hygiene issues will be addressed during food preparation events.

Infants can help mash cooked pumpkin pieces and toddlers can mash ripe bananas with forks and combine other ingredients for milkshakes. See page 80 for individual and group recipes that children can prepare with the support of staff and parents.

Partaking

Partaking of food involves children in selecting and eating a variety of food in a variety of settings. Children can be involved in the presentation of the food and in serving themselves. They can learn about cultural similarities and differences through tasting different foods and using different utensils in different settings. Eating food can be a large social event, such as lunch in the center or it could be an intimate snack of cheese and raisins in the Housekeeping Center. Approach 6 (page 79) includes further discussion of selecting and presenting foods.

Different settings for meals

Meals can be served family-style with cups, plates, and cutlery at each place. Food can be passed around in small containers and children can serve themselves. For a change of place, children could have a picnic and sit on a rug outdoors, at a nearby park, or even in the center. If an Asian meal is served, children can eat with chopsticks, using bowls and sitting on the floor at a low table. Some meals can be eaten with freshly washed fingers. Soup can be served in a cup or a bowl and sipped or eaten with a metal or ceramic spoon.

As often as possible, adults should sit with children during meal times and share the social experience. With practice, children can gain skills in selecting their own food and choosing how much to eat.

It is important that children are introduced to a wide variety of foods. When programs provide meals, menus can be planned to provide a wide variety. Children also like routines, so it is great to repeat popular meals on a regular basis along with new or unique foods. If children bring their own meals, there may be opportunities for discussing the different foods brought from home. Parents can be encouraged to provide a variety of different lunches and snacks. Children may help prepare meals at home and while at the center. See page 134 for suggestions about planning meals (Chapter 4 Section 4).

Washing up and cleaning up are often very popular experiences for young children. They are a very important part of partaking of food.

Processing wastes

Processing wastes from any food preparation or eating experience might include feeding stale bread and vegetable scraps to chickens, composting food scraps for gardening, recycling aluminium cans and glass bottles, or feeding newspaper and plant scraps to a worm farm. Chicken manure can be recycled as a natural fertilizer for gardens.

Recycling

Recycling programs work best when the whole community or family is involved. Many local government authorities now have recycling programs for reusing materials such as aluminium, tin, paper, glass, and plastic. Raising awareness of these programs in early childhood programs can help to raise awareness at home.

Conservation

Practices such as taking cloth shopping bags to the supermarket for groceries or at least reducing the number of plastic bags brought home (ask the cashier to fill them as full as possible without breaking) can help reduce the amount of waste plastic. Also look for products with little or no packaging—there is no reason soap has to be wrapped in cardboard, paper, and cellophane!

Compost

There are many ways of producing compost from household and garden scraps. One method of doing this is described below. A compost bin is an efficient way for turning organic waste into cheap mulch and fertilizer for gardening experiences.

You will need a black plastic garbage bin with high carbon waste (leaves, paper/cardboard, sawdust, straw) and high nitrogen waste (animal manure except from a dog or cat, food scraps, lawn clippings). It is best to have more high carbon waste than high nitrogen waste. The balance of wet and dry is important too—not too damp or too dry!

Cut the bottom out of the bin to allow direct contact with the soil.

Layer organic materials into the bin. A wide variety of different materials is important. Thin layers of soil now and then will help prevent the material from becoming sloppy and also provide extra microbes to help make your compost work.

When the bin is full, cover the materials with a layer of soil and close the lid. Leave the lid on for at least two weeks and then place another

layer of soil on top. Close the bin for another six weeks. After this, the compost may be ready to put into your garden or add to gardening containers. The waste-to-resource process time will vary with seasonal changes as well as temperature and moisture levels.

Approach 4

Language, drama, and social studies

SIX APPROACHES TO FOOD LEARNING THROUGH LANGUAGE, DRAMA, AND SOCIAL STUDIES

> Books, literature.

> Home and community.

> Food from around the world.

> Drawing and writing.

> Music.

> Dramatic play.

Many children's books revolve around issues and contexts of food. Books are one great starting point for food experiences. They can heighten children's awareness of their own home and local community and also introduce them to worlds outside their own experiences.

Children as young as two years can dramatize these stories, and many four- and five-year-olds can retell stories using representations of the characters and other story elements made from felt or another medium. Children can make up their own stories. They can write or draw about their own food experiences and then dramatize the stories. Music, song, and dance add other dimensions to these experiences. There are many songs, poems, and fingerplays about food that young children will enjoy.

Curriculum webs of children's books

Curriculum webs are one form of planning for children's learning. A web of concepts, topics, or learning experiences is really a brainstormed array of possibilities that adults and children can jointly contribute to and select from (Workman and Anziano, 1993). A web can incorporate various teaching styles and modes of learning for children. A web can be cross-curriculum and focus on similar levels of development and past experiences of broader and varied ages and interests of children.

Curriculum webs have been designed with several well-known children's books as a starting point. These books have been selected to address a wide range of food issues and represent a variety of genres. This is by no means an exhaustive list and there are many more excellent children's books, both factual and fiction, that could be used (Bromley, 1995). The webs provide topics for discussion and a variety of learning experiences that can be developed depending on the ages, past experiences, and current interests of the children. Each experience can be undertaken separately or linked as part of a project or topic approach to learning. It is certainly not expected that all web components would be addressed at one time or even sequentially. Learning experiences can be child-initiated and most include hands-on involvement of children, while some are more teacher-led or modeled. The majority of these learning experiences allow several children to participate as a group, however, some might involve only two or three children with an adult in one corner or a learning center of the room. A group of children need not participate as a whole, nor necessarily participate on that day. You are encouraged to modify these experiences for different settings and specific children's interests and needs.

Sharing books with children by Beverley Broughton

Books provide a powerful means of engaging children's thinking and feelings about a topic. In reading and listening to stories with their teacher, children are involved in meaning-making through:

▶ interpreting and making sense of information; and

▶ connecting it with their prior understandings about and attitudes towards the topic and theme of the story.

The process of interactive story reading facilitates the sharing of ideas through dialogue and discussion. Opportunities for prediction about the story prior to reading it stimulates children's knowledge and expectations, and brief interchanges during story reading maintain their involvement. After the story has been read, talking about the book helps children understand its messages. In these conversations, children are encouraged to express their own interpretations, listen to those of others, and make links with prior knowledge and experiences. The teacher's role is to encourage contributions, clarify and guide understanding through sensitive questioning, and provide additional information.

Children can extend their understandings by "revisiting" stories, hearing them again, or through selecting them for personal choice reading, perhaps with a friend.

Used like this, books can contribute to a sense of community within the group, which is the ideal context for follow-up collaborative learning opportunities for all young children.

Beverley Broughton is lecturer in literary education and children's literature, School of Early Childhood, QUT.

Several examples of curriculum webs for the following children's books appear on the next few pages:

The Little Red Hen by Paul Galodone

Scallywag by Jeannette Rowe

The Carrot Seed by Ruth Krauss

Goldilocks and the Three Bears retold by Jan Brett

Growing Vegetable Soup by Lois Ehlert

The Very Hungry Caterpillar by Eric Carle

Let's Eat! by Ana Zamorano

Wombat Stew by Marcia Vaugh

Look at pictures with infants and toddlers, label the scenes, handle feathers.

Encourage children to act out the story with puppets or props. What happened in the story? Why did the characters make these choices?

Collect different types of edible seeds. These and wheat heads can be displayed. As a sensory experience, collect a big container full of one type of seed for children to feel, play with, and run their fingers through. Add smaller containers for pouring and measuring. Where do the different seeds come from?

Children can practice decision-making. They can help organize a breakfast at the center with lots of grain foods. What will the menu be? Shop for ingredients. Help prepare the foods. Invite special guests.

Bake bread together. Allow the children to help measure, mix, pour, knead, and so on. Bake it and cut it, then each child can make a sandwich for lunch from a choice of fillings.

The Little Red Hen

by Paul Galdone

Provide materials for a bakery if the children wish to play act.

Other ideas?

Read *The Giant Jam Sandwich* by John Vernon Lord. Make sequence cards of the story. The children can then arrange the cards to retell the story.

Sprout wheat seeds. Plant the seedlings in soil and monitor their growth. Talk about what is made from wheat.

Song: "Oats, peas, beans"

What is yeast? Why is it mixed into bread? Make bread with and without yeast. Explore the scientific process—predict, experiment, record your findings.

Use pictures of a wheat farm and processes involved in producing the crop, milling the flour, and baking with it.

What is the difference between whole wheat and white bread flour? Which do you like the best? Why?

What sort of food does your pet like? How often do you feed him or her? What do you do with leftovers or scraps?

What things do we need to do to keep our heart, teeth, and the rest of our bodies healthy? A dentist and dietitian/nutritionist could talk to the children about this.

Talk about the cat's activities during the day. Is he an active cat? The more active we are, the more food we need for energy. What activity and exercise do you do each day? What activities make you the hungriest?

Why do some people go on diets? What sorts of foods do people eat on their diets? What foods do they avoid? Why was the cat put on a diet? Why did he run away again?

Other ideas?

The cat in the story was very fond of cheese for a snack. How do you make cheese?

What sorts of foods do you like for snack, dinner, breakfast, and lunch? Why? Who decides what you eat?

Scallywag

by Jeanette Rowe

Make soft cheese. Warm some milk, stir in lemon juice, separate the curds using cheesecloth, and drip dry. Flavor with herbs, if desired.

Talk about where meals and snacks are eaten. For example, Bert eats breakfast on his porch. Where do you eat breakfast? Where do you eat lunch and snack?

Keep an extra meal aside over a whole day and make up the meals a child would have at home. This way the children can see how much food they eat in a whole day.

Make up sequence cards of the story for children to put in order and retell the story.

What happens if you don't eat? Look at pictures of malnourished children. Discuss what happens. Talk about how we need the nutrients in food to make and repair our bodies. Could we help these children out in any way? The center could sponsor a child in a Third World country.

Children could tell parents about a new food they have tasted or made in the center and would like to try. Perhaps the recipe could be sent home. This is the beginning of advocacy about food issues.

Read other stories about vegetables (for example, *Jamie O'Rourke and the Big Potato* by Tomie dePaola).

Make carrot soup from the carrots grown at the center. Wash, chop, and cook the vegetables. Use a picture recipe for the children to follow.

Try other root vegetables, such as turnips, potatoes, or beets.

When is the best time of year to plant carrot seeds? Talk about the different seasons. Why don't carrots grow very well if they are planted in the wrong season?

Other ideas?

The Carrot Seed

by Ruth Krauss

Read *One Watermelon Seed* by Celia Barker Lottridge.

Plant some carrot seeds in pots or in the ground. Care for the plants. Help the children water, weed, and fertilize them. What happens if they don't get any water? What happens if they don't get any light?

Harvest the vegetables growing at the center. Have the children count the vegetables produced and make a book about them.

Would you like to eat carrots every day until the carrot was used up? Have you ever eaten too much of one food? What happened? What foods would you like to eat every day?

Graph the growth of carrots by having some that you can dig up each week and draw.

It's not always possible to do everything by yourself. Sometimes you may need to ask for help. For example, when preparing food, you may need to talk to an adult first about what to do, especially if you are using the stove or other appliances.

Do you really think such a big carrot could really grow? Why or why not?

Do you have porridge for breakfast? What do people in other countries have for breakfast? Prepare some international breakfast foods for the children to try.

Have you ever eaten something that is too hot? What happened? What can you do to make sure you don't burn your mouth?

Which foods are meant to be eaten hot and which ones cold or either? Children can cut out pictures of foods from magazines and glue them on large sheets of paper in the three groups—foods eaten hot, foods eaten cold, and foods that can be eaten hot or cold.

Infants and toddlers can handle three teddy bears or three wooden bowls and spoons while listening to the story.

Goldilocks and the Three Bears

retold by Jan Brett

Children can be involved in planning and preparing a breakfast at the center. What will we eat? Who will we invite? Try having breakfast at lunchtime!

Make porridge in the center. Ask each child to measure, stir, and cook his or her own ingredients for a bowl of porridge. Make sure the porridge is not too hot and not too cold, but just right—then eat it!

Talk about how young children sometimes eat less than older children and parents. Why is this?

Look at some breakfast food advertisements with children. Can we find out if what is said is true? What makes a food healthy? What are the ingredients of this food? Why do people buy this product?

Your ideas?

Provide costumes and props so the children can act out the story.

Do bears usually eat porridge? Use pictures to talk about what animals eat in the wild.

Children may like to relate stories about growing vegetables.

Pick or dig up ripe vegetables. How do we tell if they are ripe?

Sing songs and simple rhymes about vegetables (for example, "One potato, two potato").

Grow vegetables in the garden or in a pot. Prepare soil. What will we plant? Decide whether to plant seeds or small plants.

Children could make dips to serve with raw vegetables.

Older children could visit a shop that sells Asian vegetables to purchase vegetables for a stir-fry meal.

Growing Vegetable Soup

by Lois Ehlert

What vegetables have we not tasted before? Why? What are our favorite vegetables? Which don't we like? Try having a vegetable tasting instead of fruit for morning snack.

Compost fruit and vegetable scraps and put back into the garden soil.

Make a shared vegetable soup. Wash, chop, and cook vegetables. Use a picture recipe for children to follow. Ask each child to bring in one vegetable.

Graph the growth of plants and compare them with each other and with other types of plants. Photograph or draw the plants as they grow and make a book about it.

Read other books about vegetables, such as *The Carrot Seed* or *Stone Soup,* and the children can act them out.

Cook other vegetable dishes, such as pumpkin soup, stir-fry vegetables, or coleslaw. Cook mashed pumpkin for infants.

Buy and try some unusual vegetables, such as spaghetti squash, asparagus, or canned artichokes. Taste them together.

Your ideas?

Care for plants. Make a list of helpers to water, weed, and fertilize.

Compare cooked and raw fruit.

What food do you eat on a normal day for breakfast, lunch, and snack? Which of the foods that the other children eat have you not tried?

Make a hanging mobile for under two-year-olds.

Who decides what you eat and when?

Have foods ever made you sick? Why? Why do you think the caterpillar had a stomach ache?

The Very Hungry Caterpillar

by Eric Carle

Have you tried all the foods the caterpillar ate?

How do you know when you have had too much to eat?

Pretend to be a caterpillar, a cocoon, and a new butterfly with appropriate background music.

A soft toy caterpillar can be made from fabric and stockings for infants and toddlers to handle.

The children might decide to plan a meal at the center. Decide on a menu, do the shopping, and prepare the meal. Include some foods the children have not tried.

Would one apple a day be enough for you? What other foods would you like to eat?

Keep a caterpillar in the classroom. Observe what it eats and what happens. Compare the food we need with what a caterpillar needs. Compare our life cycle with that of the caterpillar.

Some fruit recipes to try: frozen fruit salad, fruit muffins, apple and pear crumble, banana smoothie, hot fruit soup, apple sauce, homemade fruit gelatin, and baked apples.

Retell the story with a focus on food from one country or culture. For example, a very hungry camel ate one date, two kebabs, three plates of tabouli, four pieces of pita bread, and so on.

Group the foods in the book into categories.

Corn is the staple of many South American diets. Discuss with the children ways they eat corn. Bring corn products into the center, such as corn on the cob, popcorn, tortillas, tacos, or corn bread so the children can see what they look like, smell like, and feel like. Cook tacos or burritos for lunch in the center.

Mama brings home a new baby girl. Plan a celebration to welcome the new baby. Decide on the food, shop, prepare, and set the table and arrange any decorations. Eat together.

Roast pollo is roast chicken in Spanish. People speak different languages. Do you know any words that are not English? Some words that are not English are quite common, such as pizza and taco. Do you know any others?

The children might like to role play the *Let's Eat!* story.

Rosa, the baby, has no teeth. She drinks milk and does not eat with the rest of the family yet. What foods are important for healthy teeth? Are there any foods that are not good for teeth?

In the story, the whole family has lunch together at the table in the kitchen. Where do you eat meals? Does your family eat together? The children set the table for lunch. Talk about the reasons it is important to wash your hands before eating. What rules about table manners are there in your house? What kinds of things does your family talk about during dinner?

Colorful paella is the best known Spanish dish outside Spain. It gets its name from the pan it is cooked in. In the story many different types of seafood are used, such as prawns, lobster, clams, mussels, and squid. Bring different types of seafood to the center so the children can see what they look and feel like. Cook it with the children to see how the seafood changes in color and then have a taste testing.

Let's Eat!

by Ann Zamorano

Create a mobile or display of baby pictures of the under two-year-olds in your program.

Mama does the cooking in the Spanish family in the story *Let's Eat!* Who does the cooking in your family? Do you help with the cooking or shopping? Which jobs do you enjoy the most? Which ones don't you like to do?

The family in the story eat lunch every day at two o'clock. What time do you eat lunch? Is it at the same time every day? What time do you have breakfast, dinner, and snack? What time do we have lunch at the center?

Talk about the different types of animals we eat. Which ones don't we eat? Do other people eat different animals than we do? What are they? Vegetarians don't eat any animals. What do they eat instead?

The children could make face masks of the animal characters. Gather props together, and the children can then dramatize the story.

Other ideas?

Dingo didn't like the taste of the wombat stew. What went into the stew that you think might have made it taste terrible? Would you like to eat this stew? Why? What kinds of ingredients would you like to put into a stew?

Wombat Stew

by Maria Vaughn

Children could look through magazines and find pictures of foods and cut them out. Then stick the pictures onto large sheets of paper in groups. Stick all the chewy foods on one sheet, crunchy foods on another, gooey foods on another, and so on. Talk about which texture the children like best.

Collect a poster of Australian animals to display and identify while reading this story with two- and three-year-olds.

Go on a field trip to a wildlife park or zoo. Find the animals from the story. Watch them feeding. What do they eat? What do they drink? If the park allows it, let the children feed the animals.

People from many different countries eat stews. Make a stew in the center. Change the flavors and liquids used to make a range of different tasting stews. For example, add garlic, herbs, canned tomatoes, zucchini, eggplant, peppers, and artichokes for a Mediterranean flavor. For an Indian flavor, add curry powder and stock, fruit, and raisins to carrots, celery, and potatoes. For a Moroccan flavor, use garlic, cumin, coriander, cinnamon, and turmeric with stock and apricot nectar or canned tomatoes with cauliflower, green beans, and pumpkin.

Curriculum webs of cultures and countries

In this section, a web of learning experiences has been woven around individual countries. It is hoped that these experiences representing cultures will be part of the day-to-day events of early childhood programs. Multicultural education is not a curriculum but part of an inclusive program. It is a commitment to equity, sensitivity, and empowerment (Whaley and Swadner, 1990). It is something that can and should be built into the everyday experiences of young children. Providing multicultural education is not about teaching facts about countries. The purpose of creating a multicultural environment is to attach positive feelings to a variety of cultural experiences so each child feels included and valued and also feels friendly and respectful towards people with different cultural and ethnic backgrounds. Children are not formally taught about other cultures, but they can become accustomed to the idea that there are many languages, lifestyles, foods, and points of view.

Ethnic food investigations are part of a multicultural early childhood environment. Food can greatly extend children's understanding and appreciation of the similarities and differences in their own world and that of other people around them. Displaying children's family pictures and travel posters is a relevant way to visually represent ethnic diversity for all ages.

If there are children or staff with differing ethnic backgrounds, it may be appropriate to begin discussions about these countries. Parents and friends are often great authentic sources of information and can be involved in helping to prepare and talk about the foods and customs from their culture or their countries of origin. If no participating children are from different countries, experiences such as those provided here may be relevant starting points for ethnic food experiences.

The topics investigated here include:

◗ China with Chopsticks;
◗ Venturing through Vietnam;
◗ Looking at Lebanon;
◗ Investigating Italy; and
◗ Inspirations from India.

China with Chopsticks

Chinese people speak Mandarin (north) or Cantonese (south). The written language is the same in both areas. Does anyone know a different language? Maybe someone's parent or friend could come in and speak Chinese (or another non-English language).

Bring Chinese fruits and vegetables to the center so the children can see what they look like, smell, touch, and taste them. Fruits include apples, bananas, oranges, papayas, pineapple, and melon. Try Chinese fruit soup. Vegetables include corn on the cob, napa lettuce, bean sprouts, snow peas, string beans, taro, Chinese cabbage, water chestnuts, and bamboo shoots.

Noodles are a favorite Chinese dish. Soup mix with Chinese noodles is easy for children to prepare. Children can also eat the noodles out of small cups with chopsticks.

Talk about Chinese food. Rice is the most common type of grain eaten. Discuss different types of rice. Chinese people eat two types of rice—long-grained and glutinous sticky rice. Do we have different rice in America? Buy some different types so the children can taste and see the differences.

Modify the game "fruit salad" to "fried vegetables" using the names of Chinese vegetables. (See page 77 for instructions for fruit salad.)

Does anyone like the taste of tea? Yum Cha is a Chinese meal where people drink tea and eat a selection of different types of food.

Read *Cleversticks* by Bernard Ashley, *Chun Ling in China* by Nance Fyson, *The Seven Chinese Brothers* by Margaret Mahy, and *The Story about Ping* by Marjorie Flack and Kurt Wiese.

Cook rice with the children. Talk about how rice grows in water. Children can then eat the rice from a Chinese bowl with chopsticks. Or children could make Chinese rice balls.

In China, oranges are presented to friends to wish them good luck. Oranges can be presented to children as a present or for some special occasion to wish them luck.

Spring rolls. Children enjoy dipping spring rolls in honey or soy sauce; they also enjoy filling and wrapping the rolls. Make the filling, let it cool, and provide small bowls of filling, beaten eggs, and wrappers for the children to wrap their own spring rolls. The deep-frying or steaming can be done by an adult.

In China, tea houses are places where friends visit and drink tea. The houses are furnished in traditional style and people usually sit on cushions around a low table. Arrange a tea house in an area of the room—add a table, cushions, teacups, teapot, placemats, and napkins. Children can make the placemats to put in the tea house. It can also be an area that displays other art objects the children have created. Show children how to set the table and serve each other tea.

Venturing through Vietnam

What did you have for breakfast this morning? Who would like to have soup for breakfast?

The Vietnamese breakfast is generally "pho" (vegetable/meat/noodle soup) or a French bread sandwich of meat and vegetables.

Other ideas?

In the countryside of Vietnam, a breakfast of xoi (pronounced soy) can be bought from the xoi seller who carries a pot of sticky rice and various "extras" to go with it. The children can grind sesame seeds and peanuts in a mortar and pestle and add sugar to make a topping to sprinkle on rice for a different taste sensation.

The mid-autumn or moon festival is celebrated by remembering the full moon fairy Hang Nga. The children could make moon cakes. Decorate the classroom with cellophane paper lanterns the children have made.

In Vietnam, going to the market is a daily task because only the people in cities have refrigerators. Which foods go bad quickly and which ones last without refrigeration?

Five flavors are basic to Vietnamese cooking—sour, bitter, sweet, salty, and spicy/hot. Have a taste-testing using lemon, vinegar, sugar, soy sauce, fish sauce, ginger, garlic, mild chilies, and onions to group the foods into different flavors.

Visit an Asian supermarket. Shop for Vietnamese food items.

If there is a willing Vietnamese parent, or if someone knows a Vietnamese chef, perhaps they could come in and cook some Vietnamese food with the children.

Rice is Vietnam's staple food. Cook rice with the children. While it is cooking, explain how rice is grown and what happens to rice when it is cooked. Alternatively, you could read a story about eating rice or eating with chopsticks. Let the children practice eating rice with chopsticks.

Bring Vietnamese fruits and vegetables to the classroom such as cassava, coconuts, mangoes, papayas (pawpaw), jackfruit, star fruit, pineapple, corn, peanuts, sugar cane, sweet potatoes, and asparagus. The children can see what they look like, smell, touch, and taste them. They can group them into fruits and vegetables. Which one is your favorite? Why?

Fruits and vegetables can be used to cook a Vietnamese dish or can be sold in a pretend Vietnamese market. The children can dress up in traditional Vietnamese costumes and hats to act out the market scene.

Looking at Lebanon

Compare Lebanese pocket bread to other types of bread. How is it different? Try it with hummus. What do you have with bread at home? The children could prepare various salad vegetables and put them in the bread pocket as a Lebanese lunch.

The Lebanese meal often ends with sweet filo pastries and syrup cakes. Make some pastry and give each child a piece to mold into shapes. Place them on a baking tray, sprinkle with sugar, and bake.

Other ideas?

Foods are traditionally eaten with the fingers and the right hand only is used for eating. For this reason many foods are on skewers, or are accompanied by pita bread to scoop them up. The children could thread cubes of meat and vegetables on skewers to make shish kebabs. Pita bread could be used to eat hummus.

The children could plant parsley seeds or plants in pots at the center. When it is ready to be picked, chop it up with tomatoes and the other ingredients to make a tabouli salad.

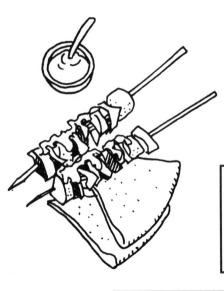

Yogurt is a common ingredient in Lebanese cooking. What is yogurt made from? Yogurt is often one of the dairy foods eaten by toddlers and older children. When do you eat yogurt? What flavor do you like? Make yogurt at the center and flavor with cut-up fruit.

Compare leavened and unleavened bread. Put yeast in half a bread mixture and leave it out of the other half. Bake it and compare the difference between the appearance and taste.

Does anyone like the taste of coffee? Lebanese people like coffee or strong, sweet tea.

Eggplant, peppers, tomatoes, zucchinis, and olives are often used in Lebanese cooking. Cut open the vegetables to compare the different insides. Cook and taste.

INVESTIGATING ITALY

Has everyone tried pizza? What do you like on the top of your pizzas? The children can be involved in planning to make a pizza in the center or watch a professional pizza maker prepare one from the beginning. Explain how pizza originated in Italy but is now a common food eaten in America. Provide other examples of traditional Italian foods that are commonly eaten by Americans, for example, lasagna and spaghetti.

Have a pasta-tasting lunch using a variety of pasta so children can taste the differences.

Set up an Italian delicatessen or grocery store where the children can pretend to buy things such as cheese, meats, olives, different types of pasta, and other foods traditionally associated with Italy.

Gelato has often been called the Italians' answer for ice cream. Try some on a hot summer day at the center or try and make your own.

Where do we store uncooked pasta? Where do we store cooked pasta? Why?

Read *Strega Nona* by Tomie dePaola. Make props for children to dramatize the story.

Tips for cooking and eating spaghetti:
1. Use a large pan with ample water. The water must be boiling before the pasta is added.
2. When adding the pasta, don't break the pasta or spaghetti but feed it in gradually.
3. Boil uncovered until pasta is cooked but still firm to bite (al dente).
4. When eating pasta or spaghetti, curl it around your fork. You can use a spoon as well if you like, but you should never cut it with a knife. If you have to suck in a straggling end, it doesn't matter.

Collect samples of as many kinds of pasta as you can find. Children can glue them to a large piece of paper and then guess what they look like. The following translations might help you identify the pasta: *spaghetti*—long, thin strings; *farfalle*—butterflies; *cappellini*—little hairs; *anelli*—little rings; *penne*—quills; *cannelloni*—big tubes; *conchiglie*—shells; *lasagna*—broad sheets; *tagliatelli* or *fettucini*—long ribbons.

Experiment with adding a cup of water to different types of pasta and leaving it overnight. Observe and feel the difference.

The children can make their own pasta. They can cut the pasta into any shape they want and compare it with the more traditional shapes. Compare taste, smell, and feel with store-bought pasta. Try with a variety of Italian sauces. There are many different varieties in the supermarket.

Rice is also commonly eaten in some parts of Italy. The children could make risotto using arborio rice. Is this different from Chinese rice?

Do Carrots Make You See Better?

Inspirations from India

Many Indian people do not use any cutlery. They eat with only their right hand. Sometimes the *puris* (a type of fried bread) can be formed into spoons. No plates are used in Southern India. Banana leaves are used instead. Traditional Indians usually sit on the floor or on cushions to eat their meals—they don't use tables or chairs. Children could try to eat in this manner.

Hinduism is the main religion in India. Because meat is forbidden to most orthodox Hindus, cheese, beans, and lentils are used for protein in many dishes.

Find as many different types of split peas and lentils as you can in the local stores. Children can name and glue some samples onto a large sheet of paper as a wall chart. Cook some of the different types so the children can observe the changes that occur during the cooking and see what they taste like.

Other ideas?

Set up an Indian market where you sell Indian lentils, spices, fruit, vegetables, flat bread, and other items typical of this culture.

Yogurt is often used in Indian cooking. Indians drink lassi, which is a yogurt drink. The children could make lassi to try ($^2/_3$ cup milk, $^1/_3$ cup plain yogurt, $2^1/_2$ teaspoons sugar).

A typical Indian Hindu meal consists of chapatis (flat bread) or rice with several vegetable dishes, yogurt, and pickles. This is sometimes called a thali. A thali is a round tray or a washed banana leaf containing a mound of steamed rice, one or two pieces of bread or puris, two vegetable dishes, a yogurt dish, some salad vegetables, a dish of lentils or beans, and tea or coffee. Set up a vegetarian thali for lunch one day.

Bread in many different forms is a staple food of northern India. Provide different types of Indian breads such as chapati, naan, puris, and papadums—they are easy and fascinating to cook. The children can see, feel, and taste the difference between the breads.

Have an Indian feast with recordings of Indian music playing, incense burning, and posters. Greet each other with *"namaste."* Sit cross-legged on the floor as you enjoy your feast of Indian foods.

"Namaste" (pronounced Na-mass-tay) is a Hindi (Indian language) greeting meaning "I'll pay my respects to the soul within you." The children can practice greeting each other in Hindi by folding their hand under their chin, bowing their head, and saying *"Namaste."*

An Indian visitor could show the children how to put on a sari so the children can dress up to practice their greetings. Children could use lengths of fabric. These might be elaborate (for example, colorful with silver thread) or plain (for example, calico).

Spices are also a major part of the Indian meal. Popular spices used include turmeric, coriander, cumin, and chili. These are the main ingredients for curry powder.

Introduce the children to different spices (for example, cinnamon, saffron, nutmeg, chili, coriander, cumin, cardamom). Ask them how many they have tasted. Let them grind some of the spices using a mortar and pestle. Have a spice-sniffing test, when the children are blindfolded.

 TAKE CARE *Note: Be careful with the chili. There may be a problem if children get it on their fingers and then lick them or get it in their eyes.*

Approach 5

Physical activities and motor skills

SIX APPROACHES TO DEVELOPING MOTOR SKILLS

> **Gross motor skills.**

> **Eye-hand coordination.**

> **Fine motor skills.**

> **Safety and hygiene.**

> **Physical activity and games.**

> **Setting the scene.**

Effective food learning experiences for young children must be tailored to their developmental skills—to their level of muscular development and to their language and math readiness abilities. Children develop at different rates, but generally, the older the children, the more sophisticated their motor skills. Capability is linked with experience and practice. Thus, it is important that children have the opportunities to use self-initiated repetition to practice newly acquired skills and to experience feelings of autonomy and success.

Physical activity should be encouraged at every opportunity. The environment should be stimulating so children can play physical games, use drama to act out stories, and practice pulling, pushing, climbing, jumping, and running. Many of the skills described here are addressed in other sections of this book. Here, they are grouped in a different way to focus on the development of numerous motor skills and physical activity.

Infants reach and grasp. They can begin feeding themselves by:
- holding a bottle or cup;
- grasping a tender broccoli floret;
- sitting with others during meals;
- maneuvering a spoon into a bowl of rice and toward their mouth; and
- clasping peas.

Toddlers and two-year-olds can learn tasks related to food by using big arm muscles and thus practicing gross motor skills. Some tasks that require these skills are:
- scrubbing potatoes and carrots;
- tearing lettuce;
- snapping beans and carrots;
- dipping vegetables in dip, cheese spread, or peanut butter;
- helping to set the table;
- wiping a table;
- helping to carry lighter, unbreakable groceries;
- helping to put away the groceries;
- digging in the garden; and
- pushing a small wheelbarrow.

Slightly older children develop more sophisticated eye-hand coordination. Many three-year-olds will practice:
- pouring milk into a cup;
- screwing the lid on a jar;
- shaking with rhythm;
- mixing the ingredients of a recipe;
- wrapping spring rolls or foil around potatoes;
- cracking an egg;
- planting seeds and seedlings; and
- drawing pictures of ingredients.

Older children exhibit more precise fine motor skills and these can be enhanced by many food opportunities, such as:

- peeling potatoes;
- rolling pastry or pasta dough;
- grating cheese;
- mashing cooked tomatoes to make sauce;
- measuring ingredients;
- cutting and chopping carefully; and
- writing and drawing about their food experiences.

When children practice these food experiences they will learn to become more autonomous, and they will feel a greater sense of achievement when they are able to complete many of the tasks without direct assistance.

Safety and hygiene are of paramount importance. Safety and hygiene rules and precautions for early childhood programs are addressed in Chapter 4. This section introduces the concepts to children so that they are aware of the basic rules and understand the reasons for the rules. It is important to set ground rules before beginning any food preparations. Children can be encouraged to develop their own rules by discussion and negotiation, and this can be displayed in pictures and simple words in a food preparation area. The staff can discuss and add any important rules that the children don't think about and mention. Foods for infants after six months of age are chosen carefully to aid their delicate digestion and avoid choking.

Physical activities and games are very important for encouraging children to undertake exercise for more than ten minutes at a time. Children need plenty of exercise so they can grow up having their own "best bodies." Safe outdoor play environments should be provided with varied opportunities to use a variety of muscles. If it is raining, dancing is great exercise, and there are several children's exercise videos that encourage exercise, and dance. Children can also dramatize story books such as those mentioned in Approach 4 on page 56.

Setting the scene and preparing foods are part of the socialization around food. There are many different settings for eating, and there is no one way to "set the scene." Children can practice motor skills and physical activity in many ways while they prepare the eating environment.

Gross motor skills—from an early age

grasping	snapping	wiping	carrying
breaking	dipping	scrubbing	digging

Recipe: Snappy salad

Children can wash lettuce leaves in a pan of water, spread them on towels, and pat them dry. They can then scrub carrots, tear the lettuce, snap snow peas and green beans, and break carrots. Add sprouts, sliced cucumber, and a little dressing, if desired.

Recipe: Baked potatoes

Scrub potatoes well and rinse in clear water. Potatoes should then be pricked to allow steam to escape. Older children can wrap potatoes in foil, or they can be put straight in the oven on a tray or directly in the microwave. Bake until soft. This may take up to an hour and a half, depending on the size of the potatoes. Eat them plain or serve with grated cheese, cottage cheese, yogurt, chopped chives, and so on.

Activity: Children can be involved in digging and preparing garden beds with shovels, forks, and rakes.

Do Carrots Make You See Better?

Eye-hand coordination—from about 3 years

mixing	spreading	pouring	shaking
planting	wrapping	juicing	watering

Recipe: Thunderstorm

Children can pour some grape juice, pineapple juice and milk into individual containers with lids. Add about 2 tablespoons of yogurt and the same amount of ice cream. Fix the lid securely and shake! Yum! Yum!

Recipe: Dips

Children can make their own dip by mixing foods from a selection of ingredients, such as natural yogurt, mashed avocado, tomato puree, mayonnaise, canned tuna, and lemon juice. Plain cracker biscuits or raw vegetables could then be spread or dipped.

Activity: Children can be involved in planting seedlings or poking holes in prepared soil, planting a seed, covering it with soil, and watering.

| peeling | cracking | mashing | cutting |
| rolling | grating | measuring | drawing |

Recipe: Portuguese tuna salad (individual serving)

Children take 1 hardboiled egg crack, peel, and chop. Chop $1/2$ of a cold boiled potato and mix with 1 tablespoon tuna. Add a small amount of oil, vinegar, and pepper to taste. Mix well before eating.

Recipe: Pizza

Children can prepare a dough with yeast or use English muffins or pita bread. They can then chop, slice, or grate the ingredients such as pepperoni, tomatoes, onions, mushrooms, olives, peppers, pineapple, and cheese. The base can be spread with tomato puree or paste and then topped with a selection of toppings. Cook in a hot oven until cheese bubbles and dough is golden.

Activity: Children can draw the story of their pizza making.

Do Carrots Make You See Better?

Safety and hygiene—examples of rules negotiated by older children

no running	heat burns
wash hands	sharp knives
dry hands	wash up
handles and cords away	adult watching

Some safety rules in the food preparation area

Do:

▶ make sure an adult is watching at all times;

▶ keep cabinet doors and drawers closed;

▶ put stools away;

▶ make sure everyone washes his or her hands;

▶ have dry hands when turning on or off switches;

▶ turn off electrical things when you have finished;

▶ keep electrical cords away from the work area;

▶ ask an adult to help when using the stove or hot plate;

▶ use a thick dry cloth or pot holder to handle hot dishes or pans;

▶ keep your free hand behind your back;

▶ turn handles inward over the stove or table;

▶ wipe up spills at once;

▶ be careful with knives; and

▶ wash up when you've finished.

Don't:

▶ prepare food without an adult being there;

▶ run in the cooking area;

▶ stand on stools to look into hot pots or pans; or

▶ feel the top of the stove or a hot plate to see if it is hot.

Do Carrots Make You See Better?

Physical activities and games

| puzzles | jumping | climbing | gardening |
| running | stepping | memory | drama |

Activity: Children could act out a food cycle. They could pretend to be the wheat seed growing into wheat and swaying in the field. They could be harvested, milled, and so on. Suitable music could be played at the same time.

Activity: Children can be involved in gardening experiences, such as digging, weeding, and pushing the wheelbarrow.

Games: Play fruit salad with older children. Children are on two teams, in two lines facing each other. On each team, each child is allocated the name of a fruit and the child facing him or her is also given the name of that fruit. When someone calls out, for example apple, the two apples run around their own team and back to their place. The first one back earns a point for the team. On a call of fruit salad, everyone runs!

Memory games: A child has a picture of something related to food on his or her forehead. Other children give clues, and the child with the picture has to guess what the picture is.

Setting the scene

set table	dry hands	chopsticks
wash hands	silverware	chairs
floor	napkins	flowers

Learning experiences

Learning experiences can include:

- moving small tables and/or chairs cooperatively;
- spreading a rug on the ground;
- wiping the table;
- washing and drying hands;
- making place mats and decorating;
- decorating the table;
- picking and arranging flowers;
- setting the table;
- setting out cups one for each person;
- folding napkins;
- recognizing names on place cards;
- food presentation;
- using chopsticks, ceramic spoons, fingers, or knives and forks;
- clearing the table after the meal;
- disposing of scraps; and
- sweeping the floor.

Do Carrots Make You See Better?

Approach 6

Food selection, preparation and presentation

Food selection

Children's eating behaviors are established very early in life, and food habits are influenced by many factors. Some of the main categories of influence on children's eating behavior are:

- their preferences—degree of liking or aversion for foods;
- physical environment—the availability of food, its smell, color, general appearance, and texture;
- social influence—the attitude of parents and peers and the influence of the media;
- familiarity—how familiar a child is with the food; and
- beliefs about food—for example, whether food is "good for you" or "healthy."

It is important that children are introduced to a wide variety of foods, and are able to eat in a pleasant, relaxed environment.

Food preparation and recipes

A selection of picture recipes designed for children to use with assistance from adults is provided here. The recipe steps are described in pictures and words. These may be photocopied and laminated or glued to cards for easy reference.

The emphasis of the recipes is to encourage children to practice as much autonomy as possible when involved with foods. Recipes include ideas for preparing food individually for themselves or collectively for a small group. To become autonomous, children may need to become familiar with procedures by repeating the process with less adult supervision each time. Of course the degree of autonomy will depend on the age and abilities of the children. There are many other excellent books with recipes for children, and some of these are listed in the reference section in Chapter 5.

Food presentation

Food has certain aesthetic characteristics, and food that is presented well certainly is more appealing. Taking time and care with food presentation indicates that food is not taken for granted. Different cultures present food in different ways, and attractive food presentation for children may be different from that for adults. There is no one way to present food. Care and creativity with food presentation can enhance skills and provide a sense of achievement.

These recipes are included on the following pages:

Mostly Meals	Snacks	Fruit Desserts
Clown roll	Banana smoothie	Baked apples
Coleslaw	Celery boat	Fruit wobbly
Egg in a basket	Chinese rice balls	**Vietnamese**
Mini pizza	Fruity muffins	Vegetable soup
Rissoles	Nutty rice cake	Stir-fried mixed vegetables
Shish kebabs	Pancakes	
Spring roll		

Clown roll

Ingredients (per child)

▶ peanut butter (or cream cheese or margarine)

▶ ¹/₂ English Muffin (or a slice of bread)

▶ selection of a variety of toppings, such as egg slices, alfalfa sprouts, cherry tomatoes, grated cheese or carrot, parsley, and sunflower seeds.

Utensils

knife for spreading

Method

Spread the peanut butter on the muffin.

Use your imagination to make a clown, yourself, or other pattern with the toppings.

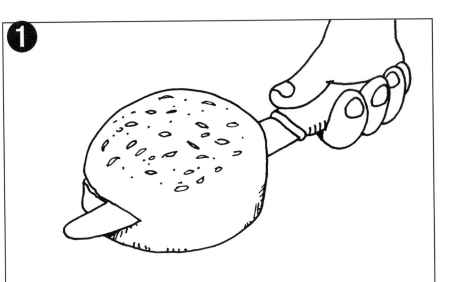

Cut an English muffin in half.

Spread with peanut butter or cream cheese.

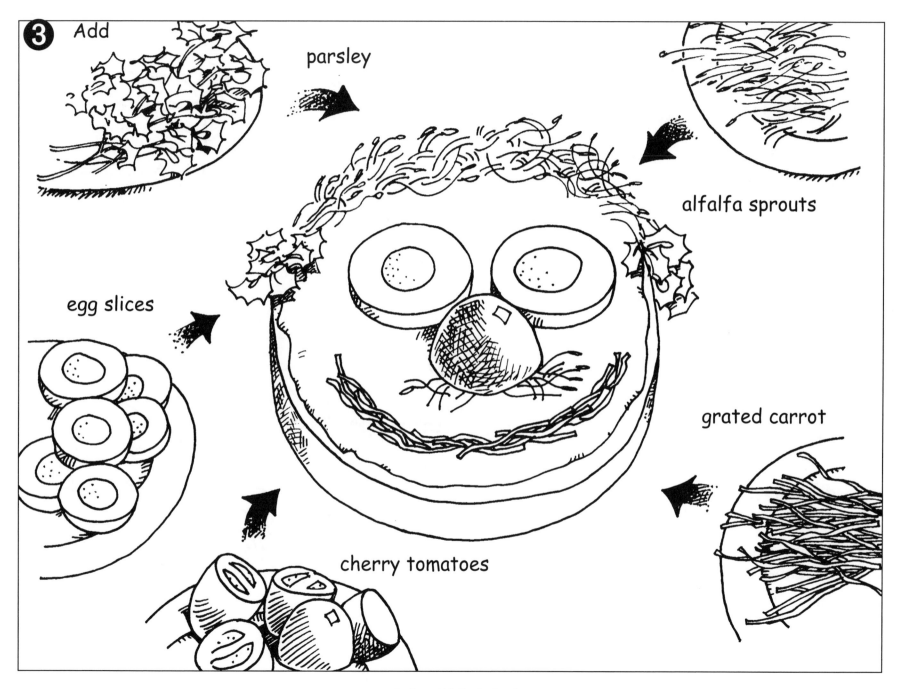

3 Add

parsley

alfalfa sprouts

egg slices

cherry tomatoes

grated carrot

Do Carrots Make You See Better?

PHOTOCOPY FOR USE

Coleslaw

Ingredients

- ▶ 2 carrots
- ▶ ¹/₂ cabbage
- ▶ 2 tablespoons plain yogurt
- ▶ 1 tablespoon lemon juice
- ▶ 2 tablespoons mayonnaise

Utensils

grater

knife for chopping

chopping board

tablespoon

Method

Grate the carrots.

Chop the cabbage.

Combine plain yogurt, lemon juice, and mayonnaise.

Mix dressing with the carrots and cabbage.

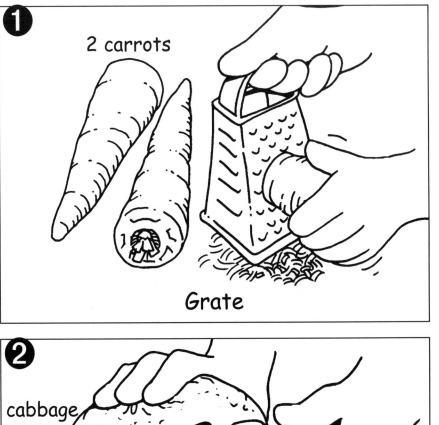

1 2 carrots

Grate

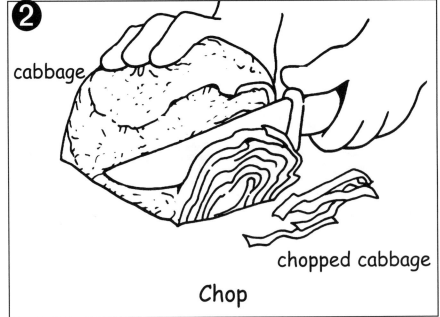

2 cabbage

chopped cabbage

Chop

Do Carrots Make You See Better?

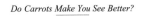

3

1 tablespoon

Plain Yogurt

Mayonnaise

2 tablespoons

2 tablespoons

Mix

4

Mix

Egg in a basket

Individual recipe

Ingredients (per child)

▶ 1 slice of bread

▶ butter

▶ 1 egg

Utensils

cookie or biscuit cutter

butter knife

frying pan with cover

spatula

cup

Method

Cut a hole in the bread with the cutter.

Butter the bread, including the cut-out piece.

Fry bread lightly on both sides.

Break the egg into a cup.

Pour the egg into the hole in the bread.

Put the cover on and wait until the egg is cooked.

Serve with the cut-out piece on the side.

1 Cut a hole in the bread with a cutter.

2 Spread butter on both sides of the bread.

Do Carrots Make You See Better?

 PHOTOCOPY FOR USE

84

3 Cook the bread until it is brown.

TAKE CARE

Flip the bread over.

4 Break an egg into a cup.

5 Pour the egg into the hole.

Put the cover on.

Wait until the egg is cooked.

6 Put the "egg in a basket" on a plate.

Do Carrots Make You See Better?

Mini pizza

Individual recipe

Spread muffin with tomato paste.

Add chopped ingredients.

Top with cheese.

Bake for 15 minutes or until cheese melts and muffin crisps.

Preheat oven to 350° F.

Ingredients (per child)

▶ tomato

▶ ham

▶ pineapple

▶ cheese

▶ ½ English muffin (or ½ bread roll or a slice of toast)

▶ tomato paste

▶ any other type of pizza topping you like

▶ children can decide the ingredients they would like on their own pizza

Utensils

knife for chopping and spreading

chopping board

grater

Method

Chop tomato, ham, and pineapple and grate cheese.

① Cut English muffin in half.

Spread with tomato paste.

Do Carrots Make You See Better?

❷

Grated cheese

Diced ham

Cubed tomato

Diced pineapple

TAKE
CARE

Bake muffin at 350° F for 15 minutes or
until cheese melts and muffin crisps.

Rissoles

Ingredients

▶ 1 onion

▶ 1 carrot

▶ 1 egg

▶ 1 teaspoon of dried herbs

▶ ³/₄ lb. ground beef

Utensils

chopping knife

chopping board

grater

fork

frying pan

Method

Chop the onion.

Wash and grate the carrot.

Lightly beat the egg with a fork.

Combine onion, carrot, beaten egg, herbs, and meat.

Shape the meat mixture into patties or rissoles.

Cook on both sides in a frying pan.

Notes

Each child can assist in the preparation.

Each child can shape his or her own patty or rissole and then cook it.

The cooking steps require adult supervision.

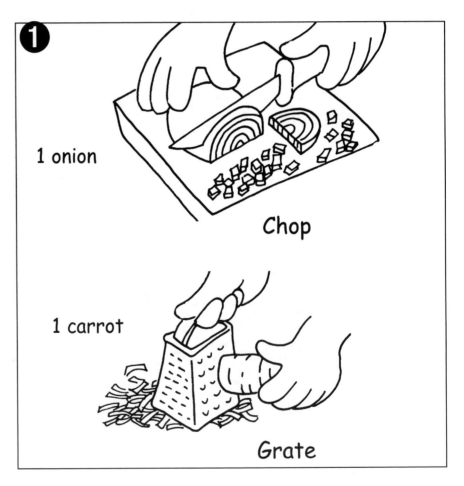

1 onion — Chop

1 carrot — Grate

Do Carrots Make You See Better?

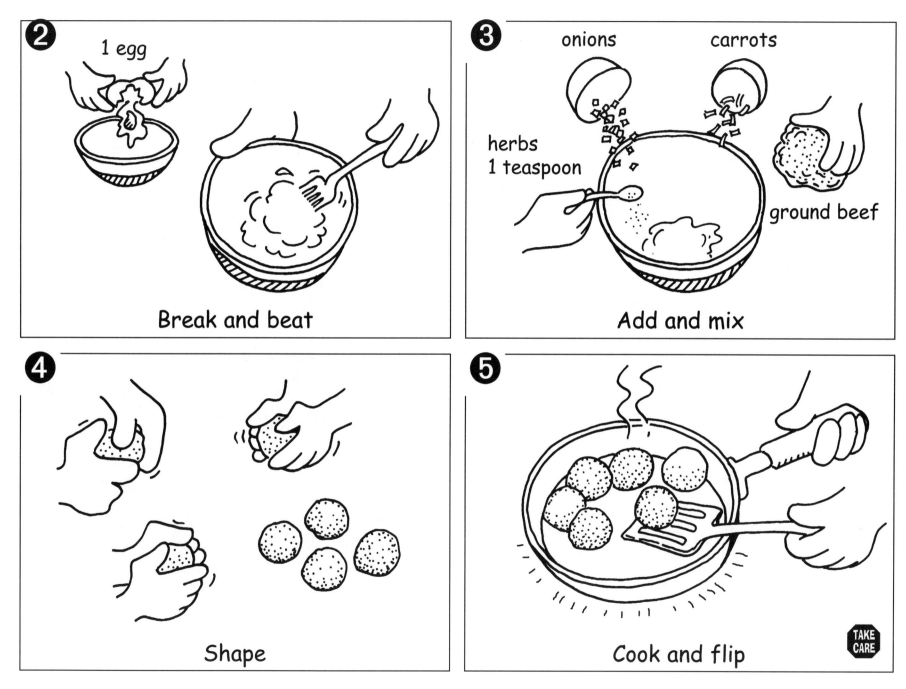

2 1 egg

Break and beat

3 onions · carrots

herbs
1 teaspoon

ground beef

Add and mix

4 Shape

5 Cook and flip

TAKE CARE

Do Carrots Make You See Better?

PHOTOCOPY FOR USE

Shish kebabs

Individual recipe

Thread lamb, peppers, onion, tomato, and pineapple onto skewers.

Grill, or cook kebabs in a lightly greased pan until cooked.

Ingredients (per child)

▶ lamb fillet

▶ pepper

▶ onion

▶ tomato

▶ pineapple (canned or fresh)

▶ Children can select desired ingredients.

Utensils

bamboo skewers

knife for chopping

chopping board

frying pan, broiler, or grill

Method

Soak the bamboo skewers in cold water to prevent them burning during cooking.

Cut lamb into 1 inch cubes.

Cut vegetables into 1 inch cubes.

Open a can of pineapple pieces or cut fresh pineapple into cubes.

Do Carrots Make You See Better?

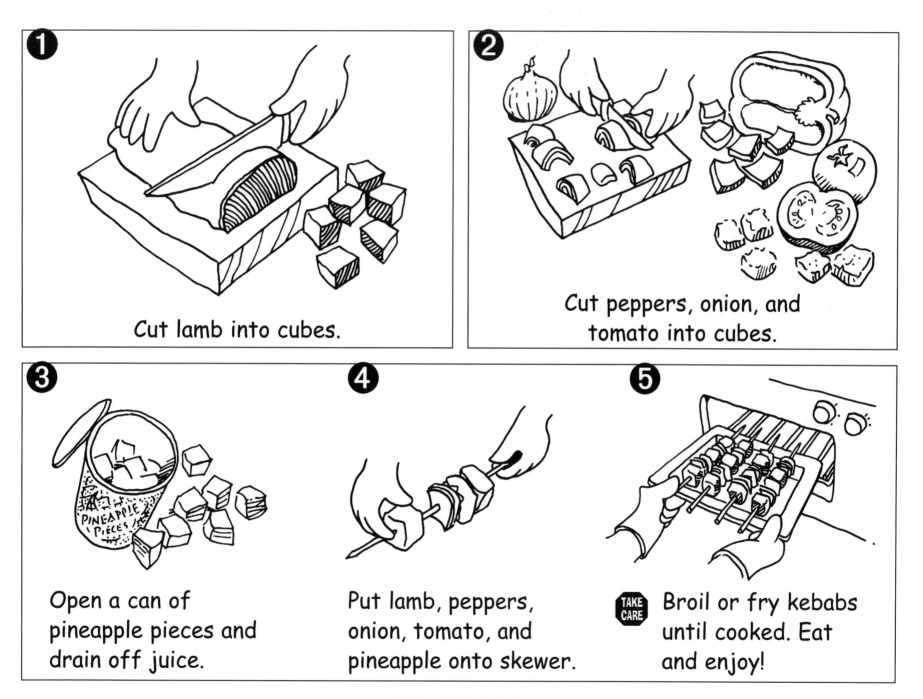

1 Cut lamb into cubes.

2 Cut peppers, onion, and tomato into cubes.

3 Open a can of pineapple pieces and drain off juice.

4 Put lamb, peppers, onion, tomato, and pineapple onto skewer.

5 TAKE CARE Broil or fry kebabs until cooked. Eat and enjoy!

Do Carrots Make You See Better?

Spring roll

Individual recipe

This is a complicated recipe, and adults should closely supervise the stir-frying.

 The deep-frying should only be done by adults—take great care with the hot oil.

Ingredients (per child)

- a little oil for frying or non-stick spray in a non-stick pan
- 1 tablespoon shredded pork or chicken
- small amount of bean sprouts, chopped celery and onion
- 1 teaspoon soy sauce
- 1 spring roll wrapper
- beaten egg
- oil for deep-frying

Utensils

wok or frying pan for stir-frying

wooden spoon to stir mixture

1 teaspoon

1 tablespoon

saucepan for deep-frying (or spring rolls can also be steamed in a steaming basket)

Method

Heat oil in frying pan or wok.

Add meat or chicken and stir-fry for 2 minutes.

Add bean sprouts, celery, onion, and soy sauce and stir-fry for 2 minutes.

Allow mixture to cool slightly.

Put about 1 tablespoon of cooked mixture into the center of the spring roll wrapper.

Roll wrapper to make a cylinder, tucking the ends in to trap the filling.

Moisten edges with beaten egg and press together.

Deep-fry rolls in oil or steam for 3 minutes or until cooked.

Drain on paper towels, then serve them when they are cool enough to handle.

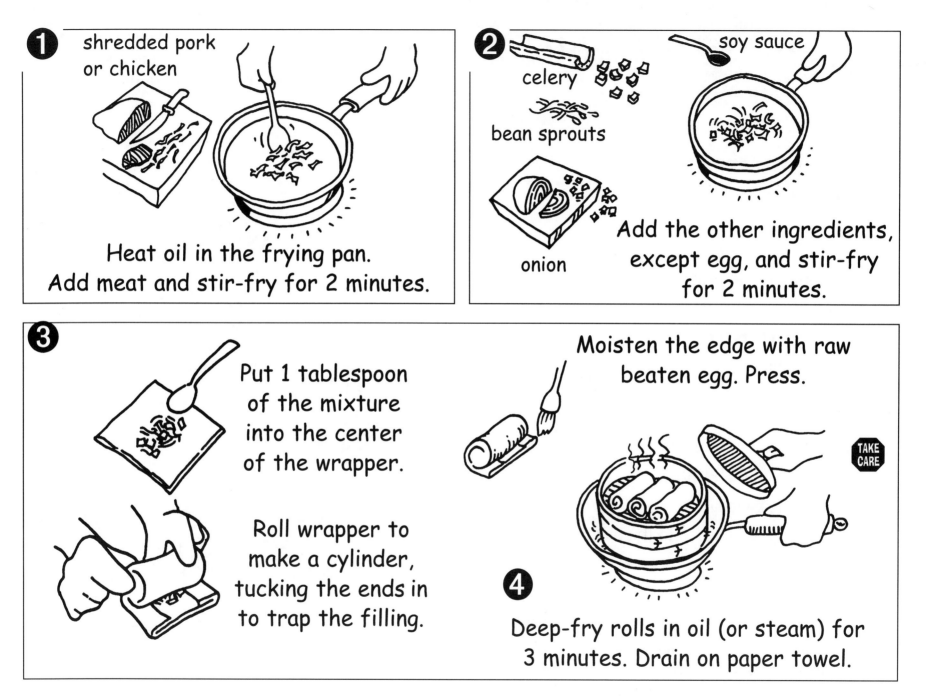

1 shredded pork or chicken

Heat oil in the frying pan.
Add meat and stir-fry for 2 minutes.

2 celery

bean sprouts

soy sauce

onion

Add the other ingredients, except egg, and stir-fry for 2 minutes.

3 Put 1 tablespoon of the mixture into the center of the wrapper.

Roll wrapper to make a cylinder, tucking the ends in to trap the filling.

Moisten the edge with raw beaten egg. Press.

TAKE CARE

4 Deep-fry rolls in oil (or steam) for 3 minutes. Drain on paper towel.

Do Carrots Make You See Better?

Banana smoothie

Individual recipe

the milk in a screw-top jar. They may then need to strain the liquid through a sieve to remove bigger lumps before drinking.

Ingredients (per child)

▶ 1 cup milk

▶ ½ banana

▶ 1 teaspoon sugar

▶ nutmeg (optional)

Utensils

knife for chopping

cutting board

blender

cup

Method

Add milk to the blender.

Chop the banana.

Add chopped banana to the blender.

Add sugar.

Blend until frothy.

Pour into a cup and sprinkle nutmeg on top.

If a blender is not available, children could mash the banana, then shake it together with

1 cup milk

Do Carrots Make You See Better?

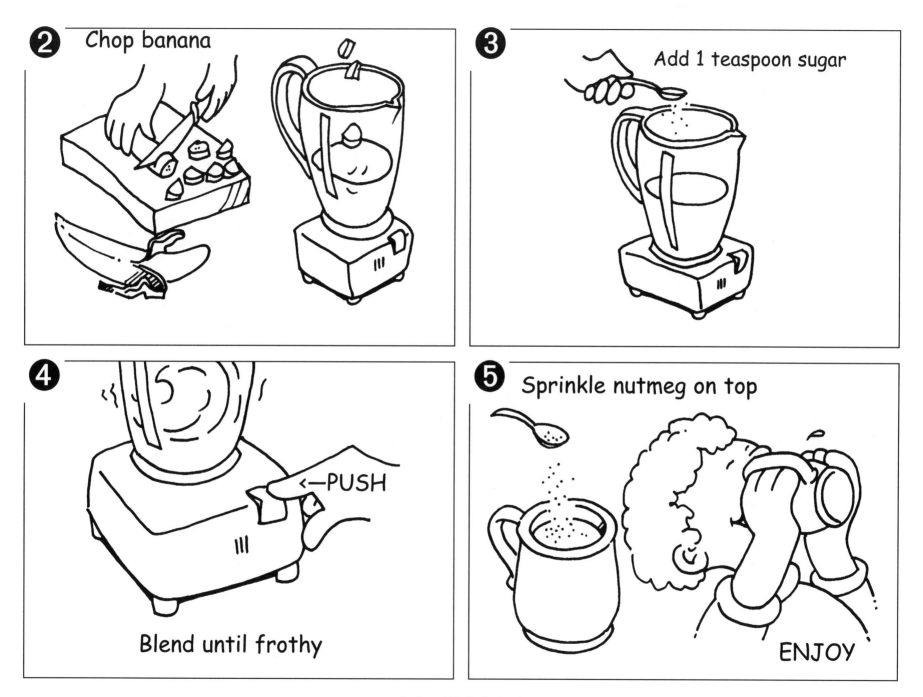

2 Chop banana

3 Add 1 teaspoon sugar

4 ←—PUSH

Blend until frothy

5 Sprinkle nutmeg on top

ENJOY

Do Carrots Make You See Better?

Celery boat

Individual recipe

Ingredients (per child)

▶ celery

▶ cottage cheese (or peanut butter)

▶ raisins

▶ diced pineapple (or raisins, chopped tomato, chopped parsley, and so on)

Utensils

small sharp knife

cutting board

Method

Cut celery into about 3 inch pieces.

Add cottage cheese to the curved hollow.

Add other chosen ingredients.

Decorate as desired.

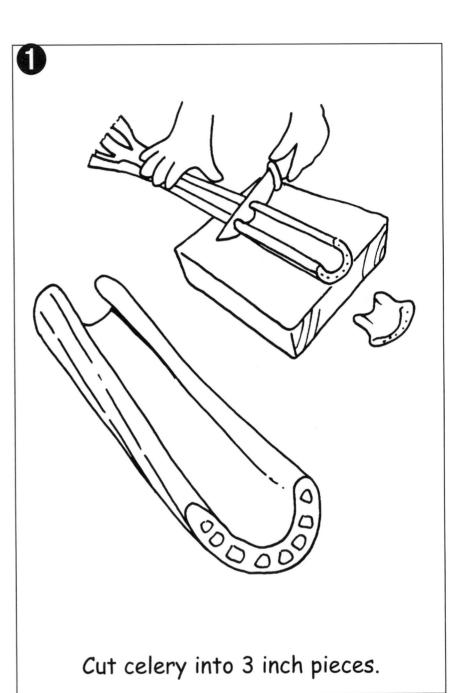

1

Cut celery into 3 inch pieces.

Do Carrots Make You See Better?

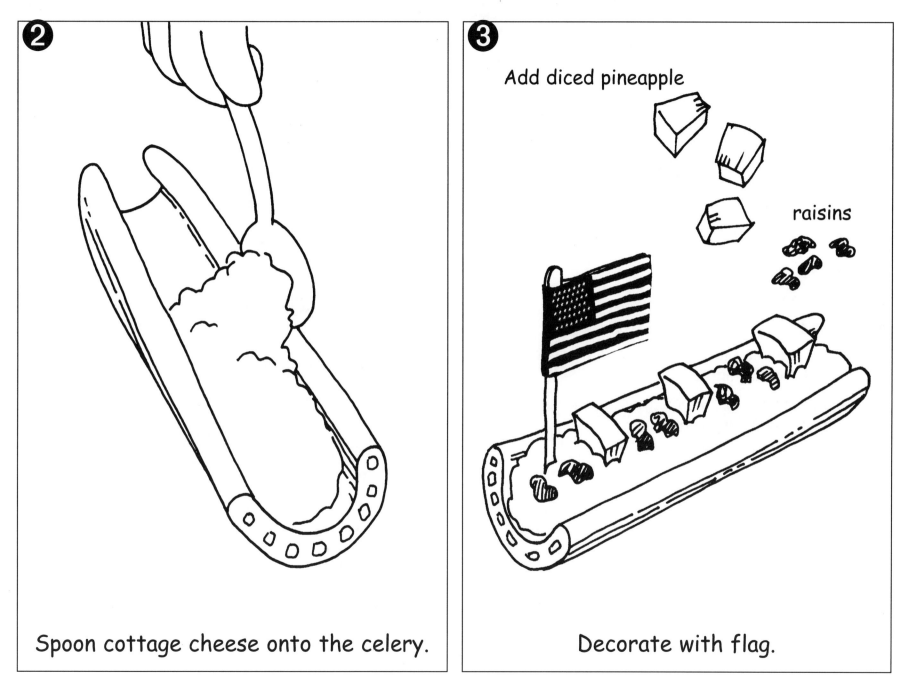

2 Spoon cottage cheese onto the celery.

3 Add diced pineapple

raisins

Decorate with flag.

Chinese rice balls

Group recipe

Ingredients

▶ 1 cup rice

▶ water

▶ sugar

Utensils

saucepan

Method

Put rice in a saucepan, cover with water, and soak for 30 minutes.

Bring water to the boil, then simmer until all water has been absorbed.

Cool for a while.

Form rice into walnut-sized balls.

Roll in sugar.

Put the rice in a pan. Add water.
Soak for 30 minutes.

Do Carrots Make You See Better?

②

TAKE CARE Bring water to a boil. Simmer until all water has been absorbed.

Cool the rice.

③

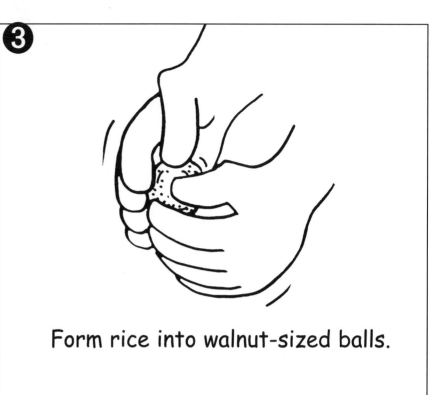

Form rice into walnut-sized balls.

Roll rice balls in sugar.

Fruity muffins

Individual recipe

(This amount makes two muffins for one child. If a group recipe is desired, increase the quantity accordingly.)

Preheat oven to 350° F.

Ingredients (per child)

- 1 cup plain flour
- $1\frac{1}{2}$ teaspoons of baking powder
- 2 tablespoons sugar
- 1 teaspoon oil
- 1 tablespoon milk
- $\frac{1}{2}$ tablespoon beaten egg
- 2 teaspoons chopped apple
- 7 raisins

Utensils

measuring cup

teaspoons

tablespoons

sieve

mixing bowl

sharp knife

paper or foil baking cups or muffin tin

Method

Sift flour and baking powder together.

Add sugar. This makes enough flour mixture for a group. Put $2\frac{1}{2}$ tablespoons of this mixture into a smaller bowl.

Into the smaller bowl, add oil, milk, and beaten egg to the flour mixture.

Stir until just mixed.

Add chopped apple and raisins.

Spoon mixture into paper or foil baking cups.

Cook 15 minutes.

1 Flour mixture

1 cup flour

$1\frac{1}{2}$ teaspoons baking powder

2 tablespoons sugar

Do Carrots Make You See Better?

2 2½ teaspoons flour mixture

1 teaspoon Oil

Milk

1 tablespoon

½ tablespoon beaten egg

Add and stir.

3 Add

2 teaspoons chopped apple

7 raisins

Stir until just mixed.

4 Spoon mixture into paper or foil baking cups.

5 TAKE CARE

Cook for 15 minutes at 350° F.

Eat.

Do Carrots Make You See Better?

Nutty rice cake

Individual recipe

Ingredients (per child)

- 1 rice cake (or English muffin)
- peanut butter
- banana
- honey

Utensils

knife for spreading and for slicing banana

chopping board

spoon

Method

Spread rice cake with peanut butter.

Slice a banana.

Add sliced banana.

Drizzle honey over it.

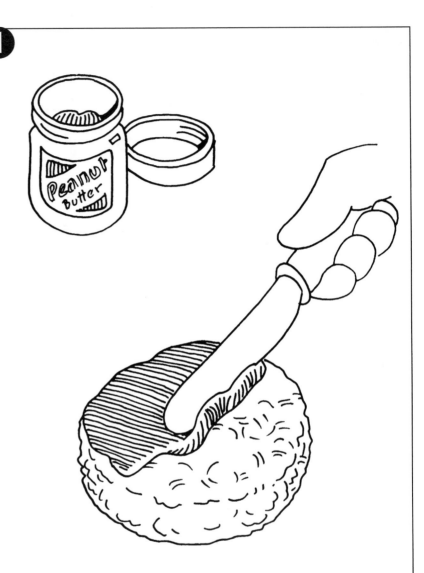

1

Spread a rice cake with
peanut butter.

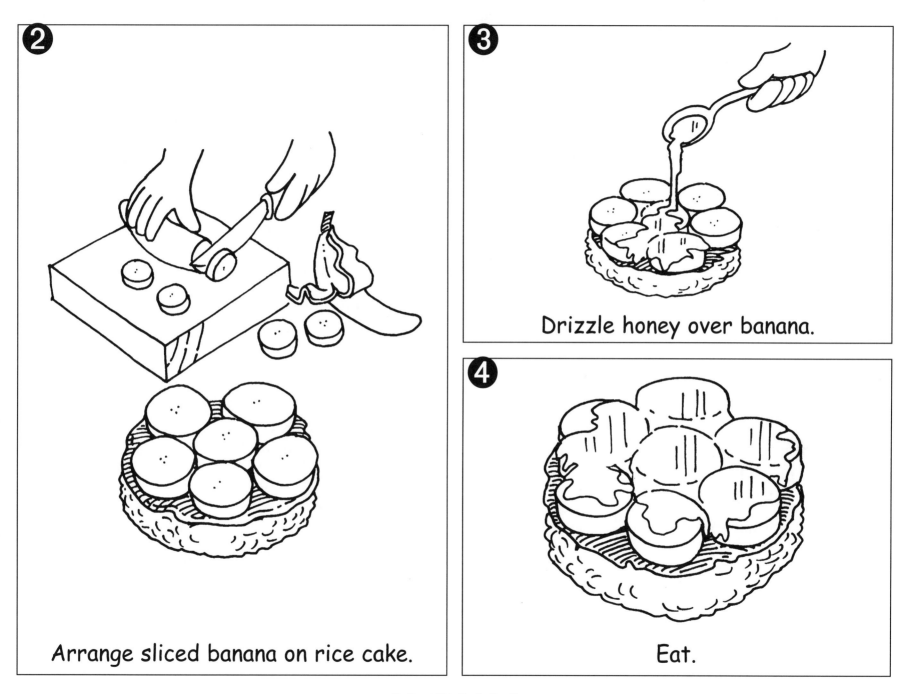

② Arrange sliced banana on rice cake.

③ Drizzle honey over banana.

④ Eat.

Pancakes

Group recipe

(Makes about 20)

Ingredients

- 1 cup self-rising flour
- 2 tablespoons sugar
- 1 egg
- ¾ cup milk
- butter for greasing pan

Utensils

measuring cup

tablespoon

mixing bowl

mixing spoon

non-stick frying pan

heat-resistant spatula

Method

Combine flour and sugar in a bowl.

Beat egg and milk together, lightly.

Add egg mixture to dry ingredients and mix until batter is smooth.

Heat frying pan, add a little butter, and drop tablespoonfuls of mixture into the pan.

Cook until the underside is golden and bubbles form on the top, then flip and cook until golden on the other side.

Notes

Each child can contribute to the preparation of the batter.

Each child can cook his or her own pancakes by dropping the mixture into the pan and then flipping the pancakes when ready.

 TAKE CARE The cooking steps require adult supervision.

Do Carrots Make You See Better?

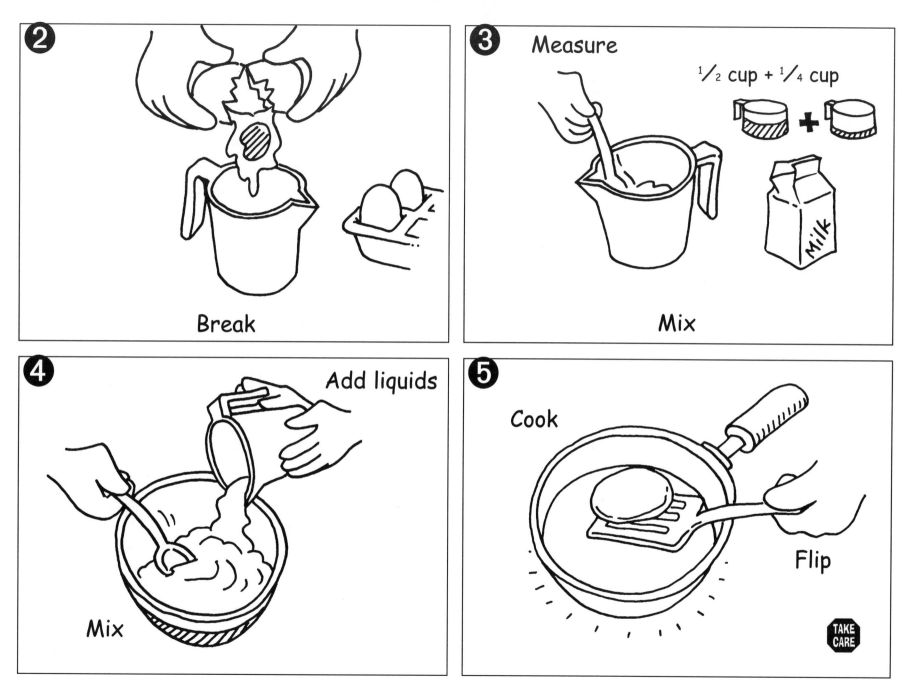

2 Break

3 Measure

$1/2$ cup + $1/4$ cup

Milk

Mix

4 Add liquids

Mix

5 Cook

Flip

TAKE CARE

Do Carrots Make You See Better?

Baked apples

Individual recipe

Ingredients (per child)

- 1 apple
- 1 tablespoon dried apricots
- ½ cup raisins
- 1 tablespoon grated lemon rind
- 1 tablespoon butter
- ½ cup brown sugar
- ½ cup water
- ½ teaspoon cinnamon

Utensils

apple corer

measuring cup

tablespoon

teaspoon

saucepan

ovenproof dish

Method

Preheat oven to 350° F.

Core apple.

Chop dried apricots.

Mix dried apricots, raisins, and lemon rind.

Stuff the mixture into cored apple and place in an ovenproof dish.

Melt together butter and brown sugar in a saucepan and then add water.

Pour mixture over the stuffed apple in the ovenproof dish.

Sprinkle with cinnamon.

Cook until soft, about 30 minutes.

Notes

TAKE CARE Adult supervision is required for coring the apple, melting ingredients, and placing the ovenproof dish in and out of the oven.

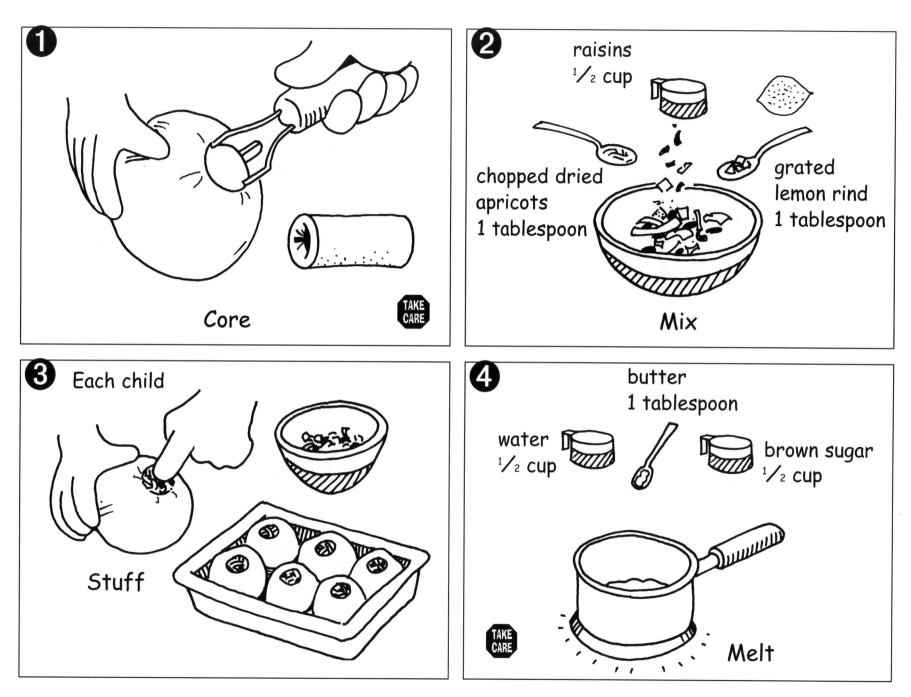

1 Core — TAKE CARE

2 raisins ¹/₂ cup · chopped dried apricots 1 tablespoon · grated lemon rind 1 tablespoon — Mix

3 Each child — Stuff

4 butter 1 tablespoon · water ¹/₂ cup · brown sugar ¹/₂ cup — TAKE CARE — Melt

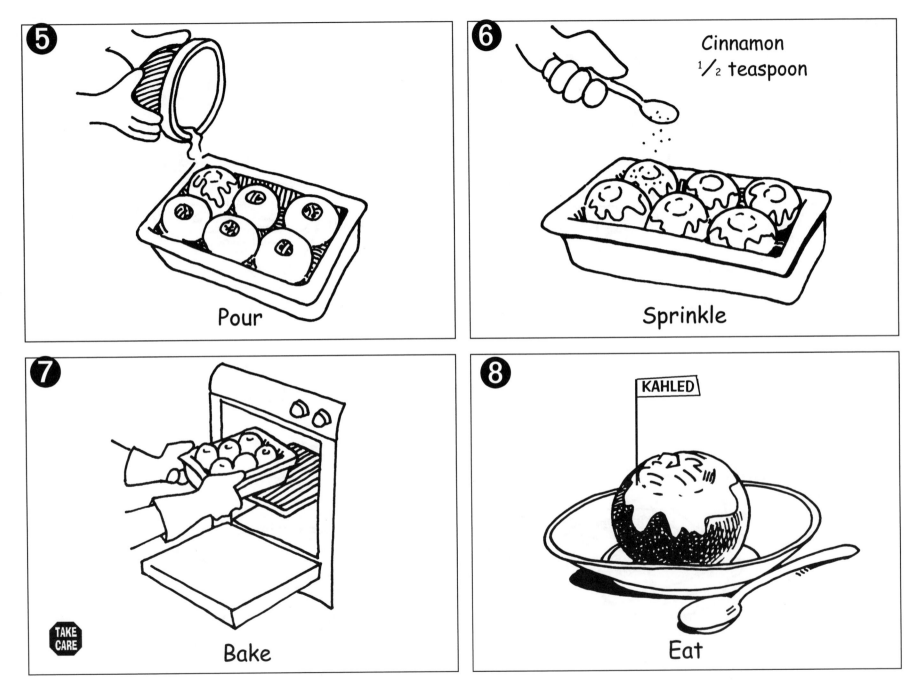

5 Pour

6 Cinnamon ½ teaspoon

Sprinkle

7 TAKE CARE

Bake

8 KAHLED

Eat

Do Carrots Make You See Better?

Fruit wobbly

Individual recipe

Ingredients

▶ gelatin and boiling water

▶ banana

▶ apple (or try other fruit, such as strawberry or chopped watermelon, but not pineapple as the gelatin may not set)

Utensils

tea kettle or saucepan for boiling water

large jug

clear plastic or unbreakable glass cup

knife for cutting fruit

cutting board

Method

Make gelatin according to the instructions on the packet (or add plain gelatin to fruit juice).

Allow it to cool.

Pour it into a cup.

Slice a banana and chop an apple or other fruit.

Add to the gelatin.

Refrigerate until set.

Make gelatin according to the instructions on the packet. Allow to cool. Pour into plastic cups.

Do Carrots Make You See Better?

2 Add sliced banana and diced apple into gelatin.

3 Refrigerate until set.

4

Canh Rau Nau Tom (Thit; Cua) (Vegetable soup with prawns or meat or crab)

Group recipe

Ingredients

- approximately 20 chives
- 1 teaspoon vegetable oil
- ¼ lb. fresh or dried prawns, shelled (large prawns should be sliced) or minced pork or chicken
- 3 teaspoons fish sauce
- 1 lb. fresh mixed or single leafy vegetables (spinach, Swiss chard, bok choy, mustard greens, zucchini, and so on.)
- 2½ - 3 cups water

Method

Chop clean vegetables into 1 - 1½ pieces. Finely chop chives.

Heat the oil in a wok or pot and add the chives; stir for 30 seconds and add prawns or meat. Add fish sauce and continue to stir for about 2 minutes.

Add water and bring to a boil. Add vegetables and return soup to a boil. It is ready to eat.

Serve with steamed plain rice or bread.

Rau Xao Chay (Stir-fried mixed vegetables)

Group recipe

Ingredients

- 6 dried Chinese mushrooms
- ½ cup water
- 1 tablespoon soy sauce
- 1 tablespoon sesame oil
- 2 tablespoons sugar
- 3 stalks celery
- ¼ medium cabbage
- 1 small bunch bok choy
- 3 spring onions
- 1 clove garlic, finely grated
- ½ teaspoon finely grated fresh ginger
- ½ cup water, extra
- 1 teaspoon cornstarch

Method

Soak dried mushrooms in hot water for 30 minutes. Remove and discard the stems. Simmer in a small saucepan with ½ cup water, soy sauce, sesame oil, and sugar until the liquid is almost all absorbed.

Slice celery diagonally into bite-sized pieces, cut vegetables and bok choy into bite-sized pieces, and spring onions into short lengths. Fry garlic and ginger in oil over medium heat for a few seconds. Add stems of vegetables and stir-fry over heat for 2 minutes. Then add the leafy parts and fry for 30 seconds. Add sauce and mushroom mixture and stir. Add water, bring to a boil, mix cornstarch with a little cold water, add to the vegetables, and boil until the mixture thickens.

Do Carrots Make You See Better?

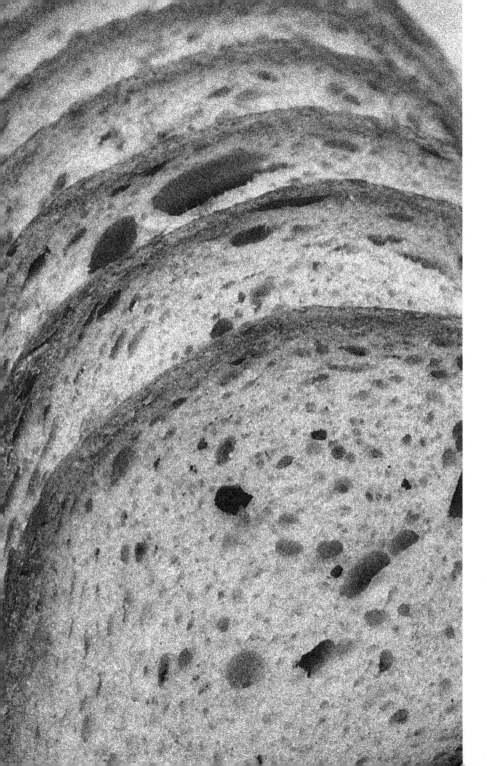

Chapter 4

Food and nutrition issues and information

Introduction

This chapter provides six sections of information, ideas, and suggestions about food and nutrition that are important in early childhood settings.

1. Nutrition guidelines and terms

Dietary guidelines for children and adolescents provide very general recommendations for young children. The USDA Food Pyramid gives an indication of the proportion and variety of food that should be eaten for a healthy diet. An alphabetical list of some common nutrition terms is provided with brief explanations.

2. Nutritional needs of infants and young children

Information about breastfeeding and bottle feeding is discussed along with the introduction of solids. There is a table showing the recommended food intake for young children while they are in early childhood settings with a sample menu to meet these needs.

3. Children with special food needs

This section addresses such issues as food allergies, food additives, lactose intolerance, and vegetarianism.

4. Meal planning

Ideas for planning meals in early childhood settings, including family child care homes, are explored.

5. Safety and food hygiene

Food safety and hygiene practices in children's programs are addressed as well as general safety in the kitchen. A planning and monitoring checklist offers an effective management tool for early childhood staff.

6. Information and ideas for parents

This section provides several examples of basic food and nutrition information that may be of specific interest to parents. The topics are formatted attractively for use as notices and in newsletters. They can be photocopied and circulated or revised for a program's individual use.

Section 1

Nutrition guidelines and terms

Dietary guidelines

This section contains general information about children's diets and their nutritional needs. It includes The USDA Food Pyramid, A Daily Guide for 2- to 6-year-olds.

Dietary Guidelines for Children and Adolescents

Dietary Guidelines for Children and Adolescents are as follows:

▶ encourage and support breastfeeding;

▶ children need appropriate food and physical activity to grow and develop normally and their growth should be checked regularly;

▶ enjoy a wide variety of nutritious foods;

▶ eat plenty of breads, cereals, vegetables (including legumes), and fruits;

▶ low-fat diets are not suitable for young children (for older children, a diet low in fat and in particular, low in saturated fat, is appropriate);

▶ encourage water as a drink;

▶ eat only moderate amounts of sugar and foods containing added sugar; and

▶ choose low-salt foods.

Guidelines on specific nutrients:

▶ eat foods containing calcium; and

▶ eat foods containing iron.

Encourage and support breastfeeding.

Breastfeeding has been placed first on the list to emphasize the importance of breast milk as the first food for infants for at least the first four to six months of life. Breast milk provides all the nutrients an infant needs, in the exact proportions, and also provides resistance to infection for the newborn baby.

Children need appropriate food and physical activity to grow and develop normally. Growth should be checked regularly.

Weight gain during childhood is an integral part of the normal process of growth and development. Foods provided to children must allow for their nutritional as well as developmental needs. Physical activity plays an important role in physical growth and the development of a wide range of skills, as well as providing a mechanism for balancing energy intake and energy output. The regular monitoring of growth is essential to determine if a child is growing normally.

Enjoy a wide variety of nutritious foods.

It is important for children to eat a variety of foods starting around the age of four to six months. This is especially important in childhood and adolescence because growth and maturation are taking place and future eating habits are being established. The consumption of a wide variety of foods makes it more likely that the diet will provide maximum contribution to health and growth and makes it less likely that excessive or inadequate amounts of any one nutrient or food will be consumed.

Eat plenty of breads, cereals, vegetables (including legumes), and fruits.

These foods provide essential nutrients. It is nutritionally important to introduce and promote these foods in the diet of infants and young children, but it must be remembered that they are bulky and have low energy density. Young children are in danger of an inadequate diet if they do not also eat energy-rich foods such as milk. For older children and adolescents, cereals, fruits, and vegetables are major contributors to the nutritional quality of the diet, particularly of complex carbohydrates, dietary fiber, and various minerals and vitamins.

Low-fat diets are not suitable for young children. For older children, a diet low in fat and in particular, low in saturated fat, is appropriate.

The guidelines on fat for healthy adults are not appropriate for infants and young children. Because of high nutrient requirements during childhood, the energy and nutrient content of children's diets must be higher than for adults. Fat is an essential part of the diet and provides a concentrated form of energy for growth and development. The limitation of fat in the diet of young children may interfere with an optimal energy intake and thus, adversely affect growth and development.

Encourage water as a drink. Alcohol is not recommended for children.

Water is essential for the maintenance of life. Without it, the body cannot function. There is concern that many of us, including children, do not drink enough water. High intakes of fruit juice have been identified as a possible cause of childhood diarrhea. Also, many of the drinks available to children are high in sugar while providing few other essential nutrients.

Alcohol consumption is not recommended for children. Alcohol is a powerful drug that impairs perception and may affect short and long-term health. Alcohol alters many facets of nutrient storage and utilization in the body. In excess, it can be toxic to cells in many organs such as the gastrointestinal tract and pancreas.

Eat only moderate amounts of sugars and foods containing added sugars.

As sugar in the diet is linked to dental decay and the possible displacement of more nutrient-dense foods, it is advisable that children not consume excessive sugar. Children have a preference for sweet foods, which means that sugar is often an attractive part of their diet. Sugar improves the palatability of a range of foods, including nutritious foods such as milk, yogurt, fruit, and breakfast cereals. Therefore, judicious use of sugar may assist in ensuring an adequate intake of energy and foods that provide a range of essential nutrients. Sugar can be eaten in moderation as part of a balanced diet.

Choose low-salt foods and use salt sparingly.

The recommendation for adults to limit salt is due to its possible link to high blood pressure in people with genetic predisposition for the disease. This guideline is applicable to children, as a liking for moderately or strongly salty flavor may be acquired as they eat salty and salted foods.

Eat foods containing calcium.

This guideline includes all infants, children, and adolescents, as dietary calcium is important in achieving peak bone mass. The best protection against bone loss and subsequent risk of fracture in older age is considered to be peak bone mass at skeletal maturity. Calcium-rich foods, such as dairy products, are important in the attainment of this peak bone mass.

Eat foods containing iron.

Iron deficiency is the most common single nutritional deficiency in both developed and developing countries. Deficiency can cause reduced resistance to infection. It may also lead to behavior changes and chronic fatigue. There are two major problems in achieving and maintaining iron balance.

First, the type of meal determines how much iron is absorbed. Although meat, fish, and poultry are good sources of iron, a significant amount of iron comes from the cereal products children consume. Vegetables and fruit containing vitamin C enhance the absorption of iron from foods such as cereals, vegetables, and legumes.

Second, some people are at greater risk of failing to achieve iron balance, because of increased iron losses (menstruation), increased needs for iron (growth), dietary choices (vegetarians), or a combination of these (for example, athletes).

The USDA Food Pyramid

The USDA Food Pyramid, A Daily Guide for 2- to 6-year-olds, (Figure 4.1) is based on recent research in nutrition and provides information about the proportions and kinds of food that we need each day to get enough of the nutrients that are essential for good health and wellbeing.

The aim of the food pyramid is to encourage the consumption of a variety of foods from each of the five core food groups every day in the proportions suggested. The pyramid is not applicable to very young children and people with special needs.

The core groups are:

1. breads, cereals, rice, and pasta;
2. vegetables and legumes;
3. fruit;
4. milk, yogurt, and cheese;
5. meat, fish, poultry, eggs, nuts and legumes.
6. fats and sweets.

These foods provide the important nutrients the body needs.

To eat a healthy diet:

1. Choose foods from each of the food groups every day.

2. Eat plenty of plant foods (bread, cereal, rice, pasta, noodles, vegetables, legumes, and fruit); moderate amounts of animal foods (milk, yogurt, cheese, meat, fish, poultry, and eggs) in the proportions shown by the food pyramid; and small amounts of fats and sweets.

Figure 4.1 The USDA Food Pyramid

3. Choose different varieties of foods from within each of the food groups from day-to-day, week-to-week, and at different times of the year.

4. Drink plenty of water.

Common nutrition terms

Below is an alphabetical list of some common nutrition terms and a brief explanation of each. This information may be useful in deciphering some of the more complicated nutrition messages that are not easy to understand. It may also be useful as a reference when talking with parents and explaining reasons for nutrition policies in early childhood programs.

Antioxidants prevent a substance combining with oxygen that would otherwise cause spoilage. Vitamins A, C, E, and beta-carotene are antioxidants. Pumpkin, cabbage, broccoli, liver, kidney, and vegetable oils are good sources of these. Butylated hydroxytoluene (BHT) and butylated hydroxyanisole (BHA) are antioxidants commonly added to fats and other foods to prevent them from becoming rancid. Some researchers believe that antioxidants will inhibit oxidation of the polyunsaturated fats in the membranes around cells, and that preventing this oxidation will slow the aging process and may prevent the initiation of cancer.

Calcium, found in milk, cheese, yogurt, and green vegetables (Figure 4.2), and other minerals, phosphorous and magnesium (found in whole grain cereals, soy products, and eggs), are needed for healthy bones and teeth.

Figure 4.2 Calcium sources

Carbohydrates are a major source of energy. There are two main sources in food: sugars (simple carbohydrate) and starches (complex carbohydrate). Both are broken down by digestion to produce glucose, which is a major source of energy. See alphabetical listing for further description of starches and sugars.

Cholesterol is a fat-like substance found in foods from animal sources. Cholesterol is also produced in the human body. Small amounts are necessary in the body, but high blood cholesterol levels have been associated with heart problems. High intakes of saturated fat have been linked to high cholesterol levels and have more impact on blood cholesterol levels than the amount of pre-formed cholesterol in foods. Reducing total fat, particularly reducing foods high in saturated fat, may reduce blood serum cholesterol levels.

Energy, in nutrition, refers to the number of calories that are released when food is used for fuel within the body. The fact that energy also means vitality, which is different from the physical use of energy in nutrition, often causes confusion. The energy from food is available to the body for physical activity, growth, and metabolism. Any excess is converted into body fat and stored for possible later use. Children have smaller stomachs than adults and must eat smaller meals more often, so that their energy intake will be sufficient for their active lives. It is important that young children eat energy-dense food—food that contains a high ratio of energy to volume. For example, cheese is an energy-dense food, but watermelon is not. One slice of processed cheese contains about the same number of calories as $1\frac{1}{2}$ cups of watermelon.

Fats are the diet's most concentrated source of energy. They also supply essential fatty acids and the fat-soluble vitamins A, D, E, and K. Stored fat can also become an energy source, but when this energy is not balanced by physical exercise, excess weight may result. Fat is an important source of energy for growth in infants and young children. Only small amounts of fat are needed in the diet of adults.

The three types of fatty acids found in fats are saturated, monounsaturated, and polyunsaturated fatty acids, which differ in their chemical structures. Most fats are a mixture of all three, but usually the predominant type is listed first on food labels. It must be recognized that it is important to decrease the total amount of fat in a diet, but fat is still an important component in the diet. It is suggested that these three types of fat are eaten in equal amount in the diet—in a ratio of 1:1:1.

Fiber (or dietary fiber) strictly speaking, is not a nutrient since it is mostly undigested by the body, but it affects the way the body absorbs and uses other nutrients. Dietary fiber is a term that covers many compounds that can be divided into two main groups: soluble and insoluble fiber. Both fibers come from plants, but soluble fiber is able to absorb water and is implicated in the reduction of blood cholesterol. It can be obtained from some fruits and vegetables, legumes, and oats. Insoluble fiber is unable to absorb water and it has more of a bulking action. It is found in breads and "bran-type" cereals. A diet rich in dietary fiber (and plenty of water) will reduce the likelihood of constipation, bowel cancer, diverticulitis, high blood cholesterol, and obesity. It also has a positive benefit in the control of blood sugar levels for diabetics. However, very high- fiber diets are not recommended for young children because they have relatively short bowels so such diets may cause diarrhea and nutrient loss.

Folic acid (folacin) is a vitamin and is important in the formation of new body cells. It is a very important vitamin for women in the period prior to conception and in the first three months of pregnancy, because it can help reduce neural tube defects in the baby. It is important for the production of red blood cells, and deficiency in folic acid may lead to anemia. White cells and platelets in the blood can also be affected. A lack of folic acid is arguably the most common vitamin deficiency on a world-wide scale. The best food sources of folic acid are chicken livers, dried yeast, yeast extract, and leafy green vegetables.

Iron is essential for the formation of red blood cells, which transport oxygen in the blood. Animal sources of iron such as liver, kidney, meat, poultry, and fish are more readily utilized than plant sources such as leafy green vegetables, whole wheat bread, breakfast cereals, and dried fruit (Figure 4.3). Foods rich in vitamin C enhance the iron absorption from cereals, vegetables, and legumes.

Figure 4.3 Some major sources of iron

Minerals do not supply energy to the body but are essential for life. Most are needed in very small amounts, and are widely distributed in different foods. It is possible to obtain adequate amounts of all essential minerals from a varied diet. Some important minerals are calcium, iron, potassium, sodium, and zinc.

Monounsaturated fats are found in avocado, olive and canola oil. This type of fat is to be encouraged because unlike saturated fats, it does not increase blood cholesterol levels. Large quantities of this type of fat have been consumed by humans for centuries with no documented adverse effects.

Niacin is a vitamin found in fish, meat, liver, legumes, peanuts, and whole grain cereals. It is necessary for the release of energy from carbohydrate foods and promotes healthy skin, nerves, and digestive tract.

Nutrients are chemicals present in food that are necessary for the proper functioning of the body. These are water, carbohydrates, protein, fat, vitamins, and minerals. Dietary fiber is another constituent of food that is not strictly a nutrient but is highly desirable in the diet.

Nutrients:
- provide energy for body processes and exercise;
- provide structural material, such as is needed by bones and muscles;
- regulate body processes; and
- are essential for life and good health.

Polyunsaturated fats are found in vegetable fats such as safflower oil, soy bean oil, and sunflower oil. This type of fat may decrease blood cholesterol levels. However, large quantities of polyunsaturated fats have not been consumed by humans in past times. Only moderate amounts of these fats are recommended.

Potassium. The mineral potassium (found in fruit, vegetables, soy products, and milk) is needed for the maintenance of soft tissues such as skin, muscles, and nerves.

Protein forms part of the structure of every cell such as muscle, blood, and bone. It is essential for growth during childhood and pregnancy and for maintenance and repair of body tissues throughout life. Foods rich in protein include meat, poultry, eggs, legumes (such as lentils and beans), fish, nuts, and milk. Moderate amounts of protein can also be obtained from cereals, bread, and some vegetables. Vegetarians especially need to ensure a wide variety of protein sources.

Recommended Daily Allowances (RDAs) are the levels of intake of essential nutrients considered, on the basis of available scientific knowledge, to be adequate to meet the known nutritional needs of practically all healthy people. The RDAs are derived from estimates of requirements for each age/gender category and incorporate generous factors to accommodate variations in absorption and metabolism. Because they therefore apply to group needs (not individual needs), RDAs exceed the actual nutrient requirements of almost all healthy persons.

Riboflavin (vitamin B2) is found in milk, cheese, yeast, liver, kidney, eggs, and cereals. It is important for the growth of new body tissues and healthy skin, hair, and eyes. It also aids in the utilization of proteins in the body.

Saturated fats are found in foods from animal sources such as butter, milk, lard, and meat fat, and in some vegetable fats, such as coconut oil and palm oil. Saturated fat may increase blood cholesterol, and a diet high in saturated fat has been implicated in heart disease and other health-related problems.

Sodium, a mineral and a component of salt, regulates body fluid balance and is important in the transmission of nerve impulses. It is found naturally in most foods, in small amounts. Large amounts can be found in most processed foods since it is used as a flavor enhancer and preservative by many manufacturers. It is not necessary to add salt when cooking or at the table. Research shows that reduced sodium levels in the diet may assist in the treatment and control of high blood pressure.

Starches (complex carbohydrates) are found in cereals, grains, vegetables (for example, potatoes and yams), and legumes. These foods also contain many other essential nutrients such as protein, vitamins, minerals, and fiber. These are not "fattening" foods, and carbohydrates provide less than half the energy of the same amount (by weight) of fat. These "starchy" foods should be eaten in preference to foods high in fat and sugar.

Sugars (simple carbohydrates) occur naturally in many foods. Examples are lactose in milk, fructose in fruit, and sucrose in granulated sugar. Sucrose is added in the processing of many foods such as cookies, candy, and soft drinks. Foods high in added sugar often contain few other nutrients.

Thiamine (vitamin B1) is found in wholegrain bread and cereals, liver, pork, meats, and nuts. It aids in the utilization of carbohydrates in the body and the normal functioning of the nervous system.

Vitamins are found in small amounts in most foods and are necessary to control vital body processes. They do not supply energy. Vitamins act primarily as regulators within the body and are essential for release of energy from foods, for tissue building, and to help the body resist disease. Because our bodies cannot make most vitamins, they must be supplied through our food. There are two groups of vitamins: fat-soluble and water-soluble. Fat-soluble vitamins are not soluble in blood, and excess of these vitamins accumulate in body fat stores. This can result in toxicity. Few people need vitamin supplements, provided they eat a well-balanced diet. Vitamin supplements may supply vitamins in inappropriate proportions. Some important vitamins are folic acid, niacin, riboflavin (vitamin B2), thiamine (vitamin B1), vitamin A, vitamin C, vitamin D, vitamin E, and vitamin K.

Vitamin A is found in liver, egg yolk, milk fat, red/orange colored fruit and vegetables, and dark green leafy vegetables (Figure 4.4). It is necessary for vision in dim light and keeps skin and mucous membranes strong to resist infection.

Figure 4.4 Some vitamin A sources

Vitamin C is found in citrus and tropical fruits and some vegetables (Figure 4.5). It is important for the growth and repair of muscle tissue, bones, teeth, and blood vessels.

Figure 4.5 Some major vitamin C sources

Vitamin D is provided by the action of sunlight on skin or from eating meat and dairy products. It regulates calcium and phosphorous metabolism, and a deficiency can result in rickets.

Vitamin E is fat-soluble and can be accumulated in the fat tissues of the body. It is required to protect red blood cells, fats, and vitamin A from being destroyed by oxidation, and maintains the stability of cell membranes. Vitamin E can be found in wheat germ, green vegetables, eggs, nuts, and tuna.

Vitamin K is a fat-soluble vitamin that can be obtained from the diet as well as from being manufactured by bacteria in the intestine. It is required to facilitate blood clotting and to maintain normal liver function. Green vegetables, carrots, mushrooms, eggs, potatoes, and legumes are all sources of vitamin K (Figure 4.6).

Figure 4.6 Some vitamin K sources

Water is an important nutrient. It is essential for life and regulates body temperature. It carries nutrients to cells and waste products away, aids digestion, and is necessary in all chemical reactions in metabolism.

Zinc is a mineral that is involved in the efficient regulation of many body functions, such as the immune system, the release of energy from nutrients, and libido. Good sources of zinc include bran, lean meat, legumes, nuts, cheese, and oysters.

Nutritional needs of infants and young children

Infant feeding

Although breastfeeding is recommended, it is not always possible and must ultimately be the parents' choice. It is not the role of early childhood staff to pass judgment on a mother's choice to breastfeed or not.

It is important that feeding times for babies are flexible. It is best to feed infants when they are hungry rather than feeding on a timed schedule.

Breastfeeding

Breastfeeding gives babies the best possible start in life. The World Health Organization recommends that all babies are exclusively breastfed for the first six months of life. The advantages of breastfeeding are:

- it helps build a close, loving bond between mother and baby;
- breast milk automatically provides the correct balance of nutrients to suit the baby's needs for the first four to six months of life and is in an easily digestible form;
- breast milk, especially the first milk (colostrum), has antibodies in it that help protect the baby from infections, diseases, allergies, and food intolerances;

- breast milk is fresh, clean, and safe; always available at the right temperature; and saves time in the preparation of formula and sterilization of bottles;
- it costs less than formula feeding;
- breastfeeding helps the mother's womb resume its normal shape faster and helps her to lose excess weight gained during pregnancy; and
- breastfeeding lessens the mother's likelihood of developing breast and cervical cancer.

Supporting breastfeeding

There are several ways that early childhood staff can support breastfeeding mothers and encourage mothers who wish to supply breast milk for their babies. Encouraging words from staff go a long way toward helping a mother who is trying to work and express breast milk.

Mothers of babies should be supported if they wish to express breast milk or to visit children's programs during breaks from work to feed their babies. Alternatively, formula can be used at the center and the baby can be breastfed at home. While breastfeeding is recommended when possible, it can be successfully combined with formula feeding—it is not necessary to feed a baby exclusively by one method or the other.

Expressed milk can be stored in a deep freezer for up to three months. After it has been defrosted, it can be stored in the refrigerator for 12 to 24 hours. It is important that bottles are labeled clearly and that breast milk left over from the day is thrown away. Do not re-freeze or re-heat leftover milk. Ask mothers to supply breast milk in multiple small quantities to prevent waste. If a child is being fed with supplied expressed breast milk, it is essential to negotiate with parents what to do if you run out of milk. Options include using boiled water or formula.

Frozen milk must be thawed quickly—but not in boiling water or it will curdle. Place the container under cold running water. Gradually allow the water to get warmer until the milk becomes liquid. Test the temperature by dropping a little milk onto your wrist. Do not warm bottles in the microwave as they distribute heat unevenly and there is a danger that the baby could be scalded. Be sure breast milk is well labeled and dated so there is no confusion as to whom it belongs.

Formula feeding

Although breastfeeding is usually best for babies, this is not always possible. A close, loving bond between mother and baby can still be formed. Many infant formulas are commercially available for bottle feeding. These formulas are made so that their nutritional contents closely resemble that of human breast milk. Cow's milk should not be substituted for formula until the baby is 12 months of age as it is not nutritionally balanced for babies. If a child is lactose intolerant, alternative soy-based formulas are available. The use of formula milk rather than breast milk is a parental choice and decision. Staff should support parental decisions. If the decision to formula feed is made, the baby will grow and develop normally.

Guidelines for formula/bottle feeding include:

- ensure that all the bottles, nipples, and utensils used for bottle feeding the baby are clean and sterilized;

- always wash your hands before handling the baby's bottles and preparing formula;

- feed the baby one of the recommended formulas;

- follow exactly the directions on the container for making up the baby's formula;

- store the baby's prepared formula in the body of the refrigerator until required (not in the door storage area);

- hold the baby close to you while bottle feeding, just as would be done when breastfeeding; and

- do not prop bottles or leave the baby unattended.

Drinks

A breastfed infant does not need extra drinks for the first few months. When babies are thirsty, offer cooled boiled water or unsweetened pure fruit juices diluted 50:50 with cooled boiled water. Make sure the baby has had the required amount of formula for the day, rather than filling up on diluted juice and thus not receiving adequate nutrients. Drinking fruit juice often (for example, several times a day) is not encouraged because it can enhance tooth decay. Also, excessive consumption of fruit juice has been reported to be the cause of chronic diarrhea in young children. Due to the risk of tooth decay, babies and young children should not be given other sweetened drinks. In bottles, soft drinks and sweetened milk greatly increase the potential for dental damage in young children.

Cow's milk should not be substituted for formula as it is not nutritionally balanced for babies, and it should not be used as a drink before the child is one year of age. Foods such as custard and yogurt, which are made from cow's milk, can be used as part of the baby's daily diet, but only in small amounts.

Introduction of solids

Solids are usually introduced to infants at about four to six months of age, but this all depends on the individual baby. The presence of certain developmental signs in babies indicate that they are approaching the time when they will need more than just breast milk or formula. The signs to look for are:
- baby is able to hold its head up;
- for the first few months of life a baby can only suck (To suck, a baby pushes the tongue forward. If the baby is still poking the tongue forward and pushing food out of the mouth when you are trying spoon-feeding, then the baby isn't ready to move onto solids yet. Wait a few days and try again.);
- chewing movements with the mouth and chewing on everything that strays near the mouth including the baby's own hands; and
- not settling after a feeding, because the baby is not yet satisfied.

Problems with starting solids too early

Because a baby's immature digestive system is capable of digesting milk only, there is a possibility that early introduction of other foods could trigger an allergic reaction.

The milk supply of breastfeeding mothers can start to reduce. If the baby is taking less breast milk because solid food is satisfying the baby's needs, less breast milk will be made and the baby will be missing out on needed nutrients.

Problems with starting solids too late

The baby's rate of growth will slow down because the baby is not getting enough nourishment to thrive.

A six-month-old baby grows at an incredible rate. To supply enough food for these needs, a baby would need to be breastfed almost continuously.

The supply of iron that a baby is born with runs out around four to six months. If extra sources of iron are not included in the baby's diet, anemia could result. Lack of iron and calories can also leave a baby prone to infection.

The baby will miss out on essential vitamins and minerals that are necessary for normal growth and development.

Even though the baby is moving onto solids, breast milk or formula will still form the basis of the baby's diet for at least the first 12 months. At first, solids should be offered after the breast or bottle. Initially, the aim is to give the baby a taste for solid foods, which should be looked upon as an educational diet only. If solids are given before milk, when the baby is ravenously hungry, too much will be eaten and the baby will not be able to drink the required amount of milk.

It is best to introduce one type of food at a time, over a period of several days just in case a baby has a food intolerance or allergy. This makes it easier to identify the offending food and avoid it until the baby is a little older. Iron-fortified baby cereal is a good first food as it is least likely to cause an allergy, and it is easy to prepare and eat. Offer only a teaspoonful at first, gradually increasing the quantity over a few days until about two tablespoons are taken. Now the baby is ready for a taste of something new. Offer a little cooked and pureed carrot or potato. Babies often dislike lumpy textures at this age.

In consultation with parents, gradually introduce a wide variety of foods in this way so the baby develops a more adventurous approach to food choices later. From four or five months, infant cereals, pureed fruits and vegetables, custard, and yogurt are suitable. From six months, pureed meats, chicken, fish, and egg yolks can be introduced. If the baby expresses a dislike for a certain food, do not force the issue, as it achieves nothing and may result in fostering a prejudice against a food for life.

Allow the natural flavors of the foods to dominate. Babies have far more sensitive taste compared with adults, so things that taste bland to us taste fine to the baby. Avoid adding salt or sugar to foods as this encourages a taste-habit for these foods.

After seven months of age, foods can be mashed rather than pureed, and at eight months, leave the food chopped. Low fat and "diet" foods are not suitable for young children. Young children and babies need more fat in their diet than adults for their rapidly growing bodies.

Young children and their nutritional needs

With some children spending up to 12,500 hours of their early life in children's programs, it is vital that they are provided with foods to meet their nutritional and social needs. The body requires certain nutrients every day to function properly. These are macronutrients, such as protein, carbohydrates and fat, as well as micronutrients such as vitamins and minerals.

It is recommended that children in early childhood settings for at least eight hours per day be provided with at least half of their daily food needs in the form of safe and appetizing foods. The other half should be provided at home before and after care. These foods should be chosen from the cereal, fruit, vegetable, meat and meat alternative, and dairy product groups. When centers provide foods, it is important to involve parents in menu planning, discuss food policies with them, and make sure they understand daily practices.

The importance of iron, calcium, and protein in the diet was discussed in an earlier section. Good food sources of these nutrients are shown below. Fats and carbohydrates are also important nutrients because they provide energy, although they have no daily recommended amounts. This is because requirements for these nutrients vary greatly in children depending on their age, size, and activity level.

Significant sources of iron, calcium and protein

Iron—Red meats, fish, poultry, shellfish, eggs, legumes, and dried fruits.

Calcium—Milk and milk products, tofu (bean curd), greens (for example, broccoli), and legumes.

Protein—Red meats, fish, poultry, eggs, milk, legumes, seeds, and nuts.

Early childhood professionals working with parents have an important role to play in helping to influence the long-term eating habits of children. Children do not instinctively know what foods are best for them and, therefore, need guidance. They need foods with good nutritional balance for the growth and development of their minds and bodies. No one food provides all nutrients, which is why it is important to eat a variety of foods each day to get all the essential nutrients.

It is not critical that children eat the exact recommended amounts of every food group each day, but over a period of time, their diet should include all food groups in the proportion recommended here. A very broad guide is provided in Table 4.1, with recommendations for

providing vitamins and minerals to meet minimum food needs of children attending early childhood programs for at least eight hours a day.

The actual amount of food required for children will vary with their age, physical activity, and individual characteristics. Children should be allowed to eat when hungry and stop eating when full. They should not eat for emotional reasons, to please others, or to gain attention. They should enjoy foods and eating and not feel guilty about how much, how little, or what they eat. A sample daily menu is in Table 4.2 (page 128).

Table 4.1 Daily minimum servings for young children while in early childhood programs (8+ hours)

Food	Serving size	Number of servings
Breads (serve a variety) and cereals	1 slice bread $\frac{1}{2}$ cup cereal $\frac{1}{3}$ cup cooked rice $\frac{1}{2}$ cup cooked pasta 2 dry crackers	2 servings
Vegetables	$\frac{1}{2}$ cup vegetables 1 cup salad	1 serving
Fruits (try different kinds)	1 piece of fruit $\frac{1}{2}$ cup canned fruit	1 serving
Dairy foods (whole fat)	1 small cup milk 1 inch cube cheese ½ cup yogurt ½ cup custard	3 servings
Meat and alternatives	1½ oz meat, chicken or fish 1 egg $\frac{1}{3}$ cup legumes	1 serving

Table 4.2 A sample menu for children's programs

Morning snack	½ cup (small cup) milk 1 piece fruit
Lunch	Sandwich with cheese, chicken, ham, tuna, or egg Vegetable pieces Water OR Lasagna and salad Banana custard Water
Afternoon snack	Butter cookie ½ cup milk

Remember this is only half the required amount of food for a day. A similar amount of food should be eaten at home, divided between breakfast and dinner. Also remember this is a very broad guide and actual amounts eaten will vary from day to day and with children's ages, appetites, activities, and other factors as previouly discussed.

Section 3

Children with special food needs

It seems that an increasing proportion of children require "special foods" or a "special diet" due to certain disorders or family beliefs. It is important that early childhood staff have an understanding of these issues so that they can answer parents' questions or be involved in a child's treatment. This section outlines several common dietary issues affecting children. These issues are food allergy/intolerance/aversion and hyperactivity, lactose intolerance, diabetes, and vegetarianism. Early childhood staff and parents should be encouraged to share information and responsibility for providing appropriate foods for children. The following information provides general background about each issue and how foods and diets may be involved. Further information is provided in Chapter 5.

Food chemicals and associated problems

There are many chemicals in food—some are naturally occurring and others are added. A number of these have a proposed link to problems such as asthma and hyperactivity. Studies have been conducted to determine if there is any true relationship between food chemicals and these problems; however, the results are controversial and inconclusive.

Some chemicals are added to provide an extended shelf-life and the high quality food supply to which we are accustomed. They ensure most of the foods we enjoy are available to us all year round and help maintain color, texture, flavor, and aroma. Many additives are actually derivatives of naturally occurring substances. There is some concern about the types and amounts of these substances that are added to foods. However, compared to other food-related health hazards such as food contamination, inappropriate eating habits, environmental contaminants, and naturally occurring toxins, food additives do not seem to pose a serious health risk.

The main chemical substances implicated in food chemical-induced reactions are listed below.

Amines—occur naturally in avocados, bananas, broad beans, cheese, chocolate, fermented soy products, dried and salted fish, liver, tomatoes, and yeast extracts.

Antioxidants—are added to foods to retard spoilage.

Benzoic acid—occurs naturally or as synthetic additives.

Food coloring—are added to foods to enhance the appearance of foods.

Monosodium glutamate—occurs naturally in strong cheese, meat extracts, mushrooms, soy sauce, tomatoes, wines, or yeast extracts.

Nitrites or nitrates—are added to food to preserve them.

Preservatives—includes antioxidants, benzoic acid, nitrites and nitrates, propionic acid, sorbic acid, and sulphites.

Propionic acid—is added to foods to reduce the growth of bacteria.

Salicylates—occur naturally in many fruits and vegetables, aspirin, herbs and herbal teas, nuts, seeds, spices, and tea and are added to toothpaste and various medicated creams and ointments.

Sorbic acid—is added to foods to reduce the growth of bacteria.

For further information, refer to the Reference section in Chapter 5.

There is some confusion about the identification and classification of reactions caused by food chemicals. Many behavioral problems in children are incorrectly attributed to food chemicals and these children are thought to have a "food allergy." A "food allergy" can result in severe dietary restrictions, which may be harmful to the growing child. To understand how food reactions are diagnosed and managed, it is important to know what constitutes a true "food allergy," "food intolerance," and a "food aversion" and the differences between these. The following descriptions clarify these food chemical-induced reactions.

Food allergy

Allergy is an abnormal sensitivity to a normally harmless substance that involves the body's immune system.

An allergy may be indicated by an almost immediate appearance of symptoms such as breathing difficulties, vomiting, diarrhea, eczema, and swelling of the face and neck.

Some of these symptoms may be life threatening; therefore, food allergies must be diagnosed by a doctor and treated appropriately.

Restrictive elimination diets should not be undertaken without guidance from a doctor or dietitian.

The foods most commonly implicated in food allergies include milk, eggs, nuts, fish, and wheat products.

Food intolerance

Food intolerance is a drug-like side effect induced by certain food components. (These may include natural or added food chemicals.)

Symptoms may be very similar to food allergy but with a longer onset time and may also include drowsiness, fatigue, irritability, headaches, and muscular aches and pains.

Food intolerance is difficult to diagnose because the symptoms can be caused by many other conditions.

Food chemicals implicated include salicylates, benzoates, and amines. Unlike food allergies, there may be a variety of foods that can cause food intolerance because these chemicals are in many foods.

Food aversion

Food aversion is a psychologically based avoidance or intolerance to certain foods.

Symptoms resulting from food aversion may include depression, irritability, and sleep disturbance.

As it is very difficult to determine to what extent food is the cause of the symptoms, care should be taken in removing foods from the child's diet. Children usually "grow out" of these aversions.

Hyperactivity and food additives

Even though food additives are often perceived as the cause of hyperactivity, there is little scientific evidence to substantiate this. Many active and energetic children may often be termed "hyperactive." However, clinically diagnosed hyperactive children exhibit characteristic behavior. The genuinely hyperactive child is extremely disruptive, destructive, unable to concentrate or sit still, and may hurt himself. Evidence suggests that there is a small group of children for whom a relationship between food additives and behavior exists; however, true hyperactivity is difficult to diagnose as the characteristic behaviors may also be exhibited by all children.

Food chemicals, whether natural or added, are essential to maintain the high standards of the food supply. While the debate continues on whether they do cause reactions in children, much of the evidence is unsubstantiated. There is a minority of children who may suffer true food allergies and intolerances, and provided the reactions are diagnosed accurately and managed properly, the children's diets should not be too restrictive.

Further information can be obtained from various organizations (see Chapter 5, Section Six, pages 189-190).

Lactose intolerance

Lactose is a sugar found in milk and some other dairy products. A specific enzyme, lactase, breaks down lactose into simpler sugars that the body can use. Lactose intolerance occurs when there is not enough of the lactase enzyme to break down the lactose, and as a result, lactose accumulates in the gut. The lactose passes through the intestine and goes to the large bowel unchanged, drawing water on its way. In the bowel, bacteria that are present ferment the lactose to form acids and gas. These cause the symptoms of stomach cramps, bloating, diarrhea, and gastrointestinal discomfort. This lactase deficiency needs to be diagnosed by a doctor and treatment is centered around the consumption of low-lactose products or lactose-free products. Some ethnic groups have a tendency for lactose intolerance. Some tips for lactose intolerance include:

- drink only small amounts of milk at any one time, and spread the occasions evenly throughout the day;
- drink milk with other foods, not on an empty stomach;
- products like yogurt and cheese are likely to be better tolerated than milk on its own; and
- use low-lactose milk products or calcium-enriched soy milk.

Vegetarian diets

A vegetarian is a person who does not usually consume meat products. A vegetarian's diet contains:

- fruit and vegetables;
- grain, cereals, nuts; and
- sometimes milk and dairy products and/or eggs.

There are many reasons why people become vegetarian, including health reasons, personal beliefs, and religious beliefs. As meat products (and sometimes all animal products) are excluded from the diet, care needs to be taken to ensure that a balanced and healthy diet is consumed. There is a wide variety of products available to replace meats and thus ensure that vegetarian diets are as nutritious as diets containing meat.

Vegetarian diets can be suitable for children if they are *carefully planned*. Children have small stomachs and high nutritional needs for growth. Vegetarian diets are often filling without providing much energy. Consideration must be given to energy, protein, calcium, and iron intakes if children are vegetarian. It is important for children on these diets to consume adequate amounts of all foods, especially milk (dairy or calcium-enriched soy, NOT reduced fat varieties), meat alternatives (legumes, tofu, and so on), iron and calcium-fortified cereals, dark green vegetables, along with a vitamin C source, such as citrus fruit or fruit juice. Further information on vegetarian eating can be obtained from your local dietitian.

Diabetes

Diabetes is a condition characterized by high blood sugar levels. There are several reasons for this including:

- insufficient production of insulin, the hormone needed to take sugar from the blood into the body cells; and
- sufficient insulin production, but its effect on the body cells is reduced.

Most children who have diabetes do not produce enough insulin. Therefore, their blood sugar levels must be maintained at a constant level by insulin injections at set times throughout the day or by careful dietary regulation. If insulin is necessary, it is very important to time meals with the injections so that the child's body has some blood sugar to transfer to the body cells. If the amount of insulin injected and the food consumed are miscalculated, there may be great fluctuations in the blood sugar levels, which can have adverse effects on the child's body.

A basic healthy diet in line with the USDA Dietary Guidelines is encouraged. Bread/cereals, fruit, and vegetables form the foundation of this diet. These foods should be encouraged at each mealtime.

Milk and dairy products (NOT reduced fat varieties) and meats/meat alternatives should also be included in the diet. Cakes, cookies, lollipops, chocolates, soft drinks, and so on can be eaten, but only occasionally. It is important to discuss the food needs of diabetic children with their parents. For further information contact the Juvenile Diabetes Foundation (see the section on organizations in Chapter 5) or your local dietitian.

Section 4

Meal planning

Meal planning for early childhood settings

This section contains ideas, challenges, and materials that will help teachers and parents jointly explore the multicultural nature of the United States today, discover a simple way of thinking about and sharing ideas, and use this technique of clustering to gather together food ideas. The ideas gathered include identifying different foods by food groupings, various cultures, and individual cultural foods by various daily meals. Menus can be planned by considering a number of important factors that guide the balancing of foods for young children across a week of meals. Other food issues and practices highlighted in the following pages are considered relevant for teachers and parents to explore either before or after gathering meal ideas.

Food practice ideas are introduced that will challenge teachers and parents to consider food opportunities and the social value of interactions between adults and children during meals.

The ideas and support items included here provide the strategies and processes for creating step-by-step food lists, meal combinations, and menu ideas for early childhood programs. This process is based on food variety, food group balance, food preparation alternatives, and cultural options. The social interactions and environmental aesthetics of food preparations and eating times are equally important, and require ongoing sensitive attention by adults.

With regard to identifying a varied diet as well as food preparation opportunities for children, there are many ways to extend your food ideas and practices. These include:

▶ discussing and sharing food issues and ideas with others and making lists for later use to plan food practices and complete menus;

▶ talking to parents and asking for their ideas;

▶ reviewing current nutrition guidelines and leaflets;

▶ looking at food books and cookbooks from A–Z by foods and A–Z by cultures and countries;

▶ setting up food files for A–Z by foods and A–Z by cultures and countries;

▶ collecting recipes from magazines and newspapers for preparation/testing and modifications; and

▶ networking with staff in other early childhood programs for sharing recipes, menus, and food learning experiences.

Idea 1—Clustering foods by food groups

A well-known food selection guide is the USDA Food Pyramid, which pictorially represents breads, cereals, fruits, and vegetables at the base as foods to eat most, milk and meat in the middle as foods to eat moderately, and indulgences at the tip to eat least. The food groups are:

1. breads, cereals, rice, pasta, and noodles;

2. fruit;

3. vegetables and legumes;

4. milk, yogurt, and cheese; and

5. lean meat, fish, poultry, eggs, nuts, and legumes; and

6. fats and sweets.

Tables 4.3–4.7 are examples of the many foods that belong to each food group. A wide variety of different foods from each of the core food groups should be included everyday for a healthy diet. In the following boxes, see if you can add to the food examples and prepare meals that use the foods.

Table 4.3 Breads, cereals, rice, pasta, and noodles

Breads	donuts	*Rice*
biscuit	granola bar	boiled, fried
bread roll	muffin	brown rice
bread crumbs	pancake	cereal
bread and butter	scone	creamed rice
bread pudding		ground rice
brown bread	*Flour*	rice pudding
dumpling	plain	rice salad
French toast	rice flour	rice cake
hamburger roll	self-rising	risotto
multigrain bread	whole wheat	steamed rice
pizza		white rice
pocket bread	*Pasta*	
sandwich	lasagna	*Buckwheat*
stuffing	noodles	noodles (Japanese)
toast	pasta salad	pancakes
unleavened bread	ravioli	
white bread	spaghetti	*Semolina*
whole wheat bread	tortellini	couscous
	vermicelli	
Oats		*Cornmeal*
oatmeal	*Tapioca*	cornmeal
rolled oats	pudding	polenta
Cakes and sweets	*Barley*	*Soybeans*
carrot/zucchini cakes		tofu

Table 4.4 Fruit

apple	grape	peach
apricot	honeydew melon	pear
banana	kiwi fruit	pineapple
canned fruit	lemon	plum
cantaloupe	mango	prune
cherry	mulberry	raspberry
date	orange	rhubarb
dried fruit	passionfruit	strawberry
fig	papaya	watermelon

Table 4.5 Vegetables and legumes

beans	corn	parsnip
beets	cucumber	peas
broccoli	dried vegetables	peppers
cabbage	eggplant	potato
canned vegetables	frozen vegetables	pumpkin
carrot	herbs	shallot
cauliflower	lettuce	soy beans
celery	mushroom	spinach
chick peas	onion	sprouts

Table 4.6 **Milk, yogurt, and cheese**

cheese	custard	ice cream	milk
milk desserts	milkshake	yogurt	

Table 4.7 **Lean meat, fish, poultry, eggs, nuts, and legumes**

Fish	*Game*	*Beef*	*Alternatives*
cod	quail	ground beef	chick peas
flounder	rabbit	liver	kidney beans
salmon	venison	roast	lentils
trout		round	soy beans
tuna	*Lamb*	round	
whiting	chops	sausages	
	legs	veal	
Poultry	mutton		
chicken	stew	*Pork*	
duck		bacon	
eggs		chops	
turkey		ham	
		ribs	

Idea 2—How many cultures?

The United Sates is a complex multicultural country worthy of exploration via foods. The various ethnic origins of children in your center, the local neighborhood, and the wider community could be explored in this context. Read about the historical and contemporary aspects of a culture and explore its agriculture, climate, and foods. Staff and parents can brainstorm the cultural backgrounds of children within their center, and then other countries can be added to this clustering, as well as regions within countries. Look at Figure 4.7 and see how many other cultures you can suggest.

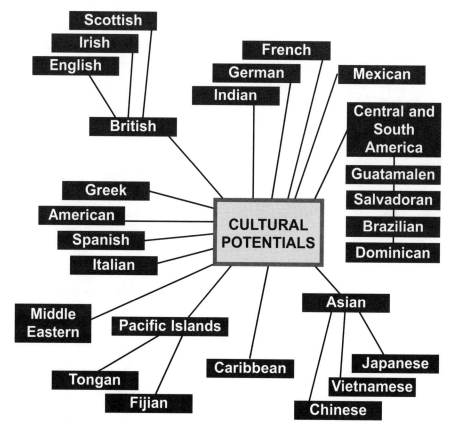

Figure 4.7 Cultural potentials

Idea 3—Gathering cultural meal ideas

You will need food references and cookbooks, pamphlets, and so on. Borrow library books, bring some from home, and use the center's staff–parent library. Design your own "Breakfast Ideas," "Morning Snack/Afternoon Snack Ideas," and "Lunch Ideas," clustering worksheets for collecting recipe ideas by cultures. For example, two people might gather breakfast ideas first from Central America, then Japan, and then England.

Arrange foods by the various meals of the day. This task can extend to copying recipes and noting their sources. However, actual recipe collection is another task. Examples of dishes are provided in Table 4.8.

Table 4.8 Examples of clustering foods from individual cultures

Chinese foods	Italian foods	Japanese foods
• *Breakfast* steamed dough soy bean milk pickled vegetables (cabbage, parsnips) steamed rice • *Morning Snack* Fruit • *Lunch* crisp shrimp cakes fried rice spring rolls tomato and egg soup • *Dinner* sweet and sour lean beef or fish noodles tofu stir-fried vegetables	• *Breakfast* uova fritte alla fontina (fried eggs with fontina cheese) • *Morning Snack* crescente (semi-sweet bread) • *Lunch* fiadone (cheese pie) lasagna minestrone ossobuco Milanese (stewed beef shin) pizza pizzoccheri di peglio (casserole of noodles and vegetables) pollo alla marengo (chicken and tomato) risotto alla valtellinese (rice, beans casserole) spaghetti bolognaise, spaghetti carbonara tortellini, ravioli • *Afternoon Snack* bicciolani di vercelli (sweet spiced biscuits) zuppa a due colori (vanilla and chocolate pudding)	• *Breakfast* dashimaki tomago (egg roll) gohan (steamed rice) • *Morning Snack* fresh fruit • *Lunch* chicken and rice with mushrooms donburi (beef, chicken, pork or seafood, onion, and egg on a bowl of rice) soup—clear, miso, clam consommé, rice broth spinach with toasted sesame seed salad • *Afternoon Snack* sekihan (red rice)

Idea 4—Arranging menus

Use the food gatherings (on the previous page) to plan a weekly menu on the "Food day-by-day" grid in Table 4.9 (see page 139). If you are using a cycle-menu or are beginning to plan one, consider not only rotating foods over several weeks but also rotate them across days of the week. The rotation of foods over weeks equals a cycle that may be two or three weeks, or better yet, four to six weeks. (This provides much more variety to the meals.) Rotation across days means that spaghetti is sometimes prepared on Mondays, sometimes Tuesdays, and so on. This rotation of days avoids the frequent repeat of a particular meal, including morning and afternoon snack, for children enrolled part-time and occasionally. Create your menus and display them in aesthetic ways on bulletin boards for sharing with all staff and parents. The display of menus is a simple yet effective way of sharing and communicating with parents. Menus can be planned by considering the following factors and balancing them across a week.

Weekly menu planning ideas

Use and incorporate:
- a variety of different foods;
- familiar and new foods;
- shapes/forms;
- raw and cooked;
- preparation styles (cooking techniques);
- seasons and climate;
- ethnic foods;
- temperatures;
- colors;
- textures; and
- tastes/flavors.

Also consider:
- food selection guides;
- the format for serving foods (table, self-serve, picnic, bag lunch);
- the time and preparation styles required;
- the costs of foods, buying, and deliveries;
- children's observations of and participation with foods;
- children's ages and any food sensitivities of children; and
- the amount of storage space required and available.

Idea 5—Meal and menu reflective journal

Establish a reflective journal where weekly entries are made about the current menu, actual meals, actions/responses of staff and children, and changes. This journal involves more than mere description—you will also interpret, analyze, reflect, state an opinion, give an alternative, provide a viewpoint ("I think ..., I believe ..., I would ..., We could ..., We should ..., Let's try ..."). Talk with parents and record their comments, impressions, and ideas. Also, design a food learning opportunities journal for recording what participative food opportunities the children have each week and note changes and new ideas for future use.

Idea 6—Display a check list, such as the one illustrated in Figure 4.8, to assist with menu planning. Refer to it daily as a reminder.

Other meal planning suggestions

Many resources include guidelines, suggestions, and practical examples of meals for children in group settings. Some resources contain a large range of recipes and menu suggestions for meals in child care.

Table 4.9 **Food day-by-day**

	Monday	Tuesday	Wednesday	Thursday	Friday
A week of variety and balance is our aim. Week of _____					
Breakfast					
Morning Snack					
Lunch					
Afternoon Snack					

Do Carrots Make You See Better?

Meal planning for young children

Vegetables and legumes

☐ The menu includes at least 1 serving of vegetables each day.

Vegetarian meals

☐ Include some vegetarian meals as part of the menu.

Breads and cereals

☐ At least 2 servings of breads and cereals are included in the menu each day.

☐ The monthly menu should include high fiber breads and cereals at least 8 times.

Fruit

☐ At least 1 serving of fruit each day.

☐ Fruit juice, if served, is diluted and is offered no more than once a day.

Snacks

☐ A choice of a fruit or vegetable and bread/cereal-based foods is available.

☐ Snacks are planned on the menu.

Milk, yogurt, and cheese

☐ 3 servings of whole fat dairy foods are provided each day.

Lean meat, fish, poultry, eggs, nuts, and legumes

☐ At least 8 servings of lean red meat are provided each 4 week cycle.

☐ Lean white meat is provided at least 6 times per month.

Also remember to:

☐ encourage children to be involved in food selection and preparation;

☐ take care with food presentation— make food look appealing;

☐ vary the place for serving food (table, picnic, self-serve) to add interest;

☐ include familiar foods on the menu and also introduce new foods;

☐ provide a selection of ethnic foods; and

☐ include a variety of cooking styles and serve both hot and cold foods.

Figure 4.8 Meal planning checklist

Do Carrots Make You See Better?

Ideas and information for family child care homes and parents

Family child care settings are quite different from full-day child care centers. The setting can often be more relaxed and flexible, and a set menu is usually not applicable.

For programs that do not prepare meals for children, parents are encouraged to provide adequate nutritious foods. Parents should be aware of providing foods from all the food groups. If a wide variety of foods is provided, then children's nutrition requirements will most likely be met. Some of the plans provided here may be useful for parents who are seeking ideas for meals to send with their children.

Food and nutrition can be closely linked with the day-to-day teaching and learning of each child. Each of the five days of the meal plan shown in Table 4.10 are provided simultaneously as experiences for children to learn motor skills, science, mathematics, language, and food groupings. As already discussed, food and nutrition education can happen during the day-to-day events of each child. These ideas may also apply to some center-based situations and may be useful for parents to see how children "helping" in the kitchen can also aid their learning and development.

 Some of the preparations involve handling of knives, can-openers, and hot equipment. Therefore, it is important to ensure that adults assist and supervise all procedures during these preparations. By incorporating these opportunities, teachers and parents can provide healthy and nutritious food while also creating a shared learning experience with children. With such food learning during day-to-day meal provision, many skills are practiced as children are involved in the preparation of meals over a whole week. Note: Water should be freely available throughout the day and with meals when another drink is not provided.

Table 4.10 Food learning in day-to-day meal provision

Meal	Activities for day 1	Application and skill required	Suggested age
One piece of fruit A glass of milk	▶ Wash fruit for morning snack ▶ Pour milk into glasses and serve	motor—hands motor—fingers/grasp eye-hand coordination	younger older
Cream cheese on toast A piece of fruit	▶ Count how many slices of bread are required ▶ Put bread in toaster ▶ Observe the result after toasting (for example, color change and texture change due to the water removed from bread during the drying process) ▶ Spread cream cheese on toast ▶ Decide how much cream cheese is required on each slice of toast ▶ Wash and chop fruit required for lunch	mathematics motor science motor decision making gross motor/fine motor	all younger all all older younger
One slice of bread with peanut butter One container of yogurt	▶ Spread peanut butter on bread ▶ Open yogurt container	motor motor—twist/pull	younger older
	Extra thinking: ▶ Name some other cheeses that you have tasted before ▶ Share comments regarding taste of cream cheese	grouping food language, senses	all all

Table 4.10 *continued*

Meal	Activities for day 2	Application and skill required	Suggested age
Celery sticks with peanut butter and raisins A glass of milk	▶ Separate, wash, and scrub celery ▶ Spread peanut butter, arrange raisins ▶ Pour milk into glass	motor motor eye-hand coordination	younger all older
Pizza on pita bread	▶ Gather utensils for making pizza (for example, grater, mixing bowl, and so on) ▶ Wash mushrooms and drain ▶ Chop ingredients (for example, mushrooms, peppers, ham, and so on) ▶ Grate cheeses ▶ Spread tomato sauce on pita bread ▶ Decorate and design your own topping for the pizza ▶ Observe the outcome after putting in the oven (for example, texture, taste, and so on) ▶ Provide information about an interesting food that originated from another country (for example, geographic location and eating habits of the country)	motor motor motor motor motor motor/decision making observing social studies	all younger older older younger all all all
One piece of fruit 2 graham crackers	▶ Wash fruit for afternoon snack ▶ Place crackers on plate, ready to serve	motor motor	younger all
	Extra thinking: ▶ Discuss different cooking methods, for example, baking pizza ▶ Children are asked to create a "pizza story" ▶ Name favorite topping for pizza	gathering information language/drawing reflecting	older all all

Table 4.10 *continued*

Meal	Activities for day 3	Application and skill required	Suggested age
Banana smoothie (milkshake)	▶ Peel the skin off the banana ▶ Slice the banana thinly into pieces ▶ Put banana in blender ▶ Measure the amount of milk or water required for blending ▶ Decide how much sugar should be added to the mixture	motor motor motor measuring/math estimating	younger older younger older all
Tomato, egg, and lettuce sandwich	▶ Spread margarine on bread ▶ Tear and wash lettuce, pat dry with towel ▶ Cut tomato into thin slices ▶ Slice the cheese ▶ Boil egg in hot water (compare the time for boiling a hard-boiled egg and soft-boiled egg, observe the difference in texture) ▶ Slice the egg ▶ Put the filling into the sandwiches ▶ Cut sandwiches into quarters	motor motor motor motor analyzing/observing science motor motor	all younger older older all older older older
Canned fruit	▶ Open can and drain the juice ▶ Talk about the difference in taste and texture between canned and fresh fruit	motor senses/analyzing	older all
	Extra thinking: ▶ Learn to use a blender	cooking skill/safety	older

Table 4.10 *continued*

Meal	Activities for day 4	Application and skill required	Suggested age
Crackers with peanut butter A glass of milk	▶ Place crackers on the plate, ready to serve ▶ Spread peanut butter on crackers ▶ Pour milk into glass	mathematics motor eye-hand coordination	younger younger older
Spaghetti with sauce, cheese, and meatballs	▶ Mix chopped meat with seasoning and spices, shape meat into meatballs ▶ Boil spaghetti, observe the change of texture before and after cooking (adult supervision required) ▶ Open jar of pasta sauce ▶ Sprinkle grated cheese on top of spaghetti, if desired ▶ Eat spaghetti with fork and spoon	motor science/observing motor decision making/motor taste/motor	older all older all all
Fruit salad A tub of yogurt	▶ Wash fruit for afternoon snack ▶ Peel and chop the fruit ▶ Sprinkle with lemon juice to avoid browning ▶ Open yogurt container and pour into fruit salad, mix well	motor motor science motor	younger older all all
	Extra thinking: ▶ Help clean up ▶ Ask the children to name their favorite pasta	motor variety of food	all all

Table 4.10 *continued*

Meal	Activities for day 5	Application and skill required	Suggested age
Dried apricots One piece of fresh fruit A glass of milk	▶ Identify different varieties and textures of fruit, such as dried apricot and a fresh apricot (talk about the process of dehydration) ▶ Pour milk into glass	science, food processing motor	all all
Tuna and cheese salad with corn, tomato, and lettuce Roll	▶ Open cans of tuna, corn, and so on ▶ Grate cheese ▶ Tear and wash lettuce leaves ▶ Cut tomato into small pieces ▶ Mix all ingredients in a large mixing bowl ▶ Spread mixture on roll	motor/processed food motor motor motor motor motor	older older younger older older all
Pancakes with jam/honey	▶ Count the number of pancakes required for afternoon snack ▶ Spread jam or honey on pancakes	mathematics motor	all all
	Extra thinking: ▶ Fishing? Catch of the day? Ask children to share fishing experiences ▶ Grow vegetables in the backyard, such as tomatoes, spring onions, lettuce, and so on	producing food food cycles	all all

Safety and food hygiene

Chapter 3, Approach 5 included safety and hygiene rules for children. It is important that children are aware of these rules and the reasons behind them. This section addresses these issues in more detail, primarily for adults.

Food poisoning

Bacteria are the biggest cause of food spoilage and food poisoning. Bacteria are found in large numbers on:
- trees, fruit, vegetables;
- birds, insects, rodents, and other animals;
- raw food such as meat, milk, and seafood;
- equipment; and
- skin, hair, and clothing of food handlers.

Their presence in the environment creates the potential for the contamination of kitchen equipment and food. In small numbers, most bacteria are relatively harmless; however, in larger numbers, some bacteria cause severe sickness in both adults and children. Like people, bacteria require specific conditions to grow and multiply. The four major requirements are food, warmth, moisture, and time.

Food spoilage and food poisoning from bacteria can be prevented if food is handled, prepared, and stored using correct food hygiene practices. Therefore, correct food hygiene practices are of the utmost importance. Food can become harmful if disease-causing bacteria are allowed to grow in the food. Food poisoning is an illness brought about by eating food that has become harmful because of contamination by bacteria. The symptoms of food poisoning depend greatly on the individual and the type of bacteria. The symptoms usually occur within 6–24 hours of eating contaminated food and include vomiting, diarrhea, stomach pains, and nausea.

Viruses can use food to transport themselves from one host to another and cause illnesses such as flu or measles. They are destroyed by the temperatures reached in normal cooking, so viral food poisoning is usually transmitted by food that has not been cooked or not cooked properly, or has been handled after cooking by someone who is a carrier of the virus.

Personal hygiene

High standards of personal hygiene are essential for all food handlers. To prevent bacteria and viruses from spreading to food, it must be assumed that everybody is a potential carrier. Here are some tips to prevent food handlers from spreading bacteria. Unclean hands are the major cause of food becoming contaminated with bacteria. The correct hand washing technique is essential to reduce the numbers of bacteria on the hands.

Hand washing
- Pre-rinse to remove dirt and grime.
- Wash in a rich lather using liquid soap and warm water.
- Brush under the nails.
- Rinse then dry with disposable hand towels or a hot air drier.

Remember: If fabric hand towels are used by everyone, these may be a reservoir of bacteria. These should be washed daily. Use paper towels if possible.

Hands should be washed:
- before and after different tasks;
- after toileting;
- after unconscious or conscious body habits (such as scratching any part of the body or clothing, blowing the nose, coughing, playing with earrings, or licking the fingers); and
- after handling raw food, particularly meat.

Cross contamination

Cross contamination not only occurs from people to food, but also from food to food. Raw food, especially meats and dairy products, contain relatively high levels of bacteria, while properly cooked food contains relatively low levels of bacteria. Therefore, if raw food comes into contact with cooked food, the cooked food will become contaminated.

To prevent cross contamination
- Wash hands after handling raw foods and before handling cooked food.
- Clean and sanitize utensils and storage containers after coming into contact with raw foods and before coming into contact with cooked foods.
- Designate separate cutting boards for raw and cooked food.
- Separate raw foods from cooked and already-processed foods when stored in freezers and refrigerators, by placing raw food on separate racks below cooked and processed foods. This will prevent any drips or falling food contaminating the cooked and processed product.

Temperature danger zone

Bacteria grow rapidly in temperatures between 40°F and 140°F making this a "danger zone." The temperatures in most kitchens are within this danger zone range.

It is, therefore, not safe to leave food at room temperature for more than two hours. To prevent food from being in the temperature danger zone:
- Thaw frozen food in the refrigerator or microwave.
- Cool hot food rapidly in the refrigerator. Divide food into smaller containers rather than storing large amounts in a single container.
- Reheat food just before serving.
- Set the refrigerator temperature between cold and coldest and do not overload the refrigerator with food.
- Large pieces of meat should be completely thawed before being cooked so the center of the food is cooked properly.

In hot climates it is important that when children bring food from home, it is stored in a cool place, preferably the refrigerator. Any food that is not eaten at the end of the day should be thrown out.

Cleaning and sanitizing

During food preparation, equipment, utensils, tableware, and work surfaces become dirty with raw and cooked food residues. If the residues are allowed to remain on these surfaces, bacteria will multiply rapidly. Food coming into contact with these surfaces will be at an increased risk of becoming spoiled and at a greater risk of causing food poisoning.

It is essential to both clean and sanitize work surfaces after use. The most common sanitizers are chlorine- or iodine-based. However, the cheapest sanitizer is hot water above 175°F. Sanitizers need contact time to work, so items should be left to soak. Read the instructions on the sanitizer package and follow them carefully.

Cleaning will remove food residues and most bacteria as shown in Figure 4.9.

From This   To This

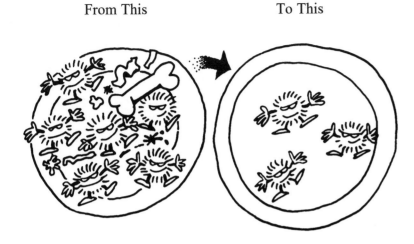

Sanitizing will destroy the remaining bacteria as follows:

From This   To This

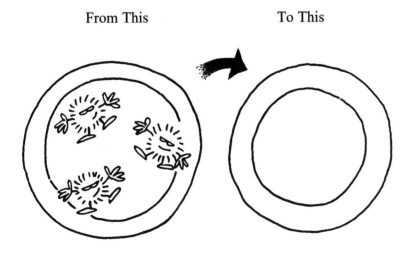

Figure 4.9 Cleaning and sanitizing

Six basic cleaning and sanitizing steps

1. Preparation (drying, scraping to remove food residues)
2. Cleaning (washing)
3. Rinsing off cleaner
4. Sanitizing
5. Final rinse
6. Drying

Note: Kitchen cloths and dishcloths are an ideal reservoir for bacteria. These should be washed daily and preferably soaked in disinfectant before washing.

Sterilizing, preparing, and cleaning infant bottles

If necessary, to prevent contamination of infant bottles by bacteria, it is essential to practice a thorough sterilizing, preparing, and cleaning process.

1. Sterilizing

It is important to know the correct hygiene practices involved in the sterilization process.

▶ Wash hands using the correct technique.
▶ Check the expiration date of chemicals.
▶ Follow directions carefully for preparing sterilizing solutions.
▶ Wash equipment to be sterilized in hot soapy water and then rinse well.
▶ Immerse equipment in the solution, with no air bubbles present, for at least one hour.
▶ Do not place the sterilizing equipment in direct sunlight, as this will affect the quality of the solution.
▶ Wash hands before taking the equipment out of the solution.
▶ Do not rinse the equipment once it has been taken out of the solution, if possible.

2. Preparing

❱ Wash hands before preparing equipment.
❱ Prepare all necessary equipment.
❱ Scald metal utensils using very hot water (175°F).
❱ Check formula expiration date.
❱ Follow instructions carefully to prepare the formula.
❱ If the formula is not to be given to the child as soon as it is prepared, store immediately in the refrigerator.

3. Cleaning

It is essential to clean bottles after each feeding.

❱ Discard remaining milk.
❱ Rinse out the bottle with cold water.
❱ Wash the bottle with hot soapy water, using a bottle brush. Also wash nipple cover and any other equipment used.
❱ Rinse bottle thoroughly.
❱ Leave it to air dry.

Remind parents to rewash the bottle with hot soapy water at home.

Pests and their control

Cockroaches, flies, and rodents are the most common kitchen pests. The presence of these pests may result in food contamination, which will put humans at risk.

To prevent these uninvited guests

❱ Pest-proof the building to prevent access.
❱ Seal off hiding places to deny shelter.
❱ Keep the building in a clean and tidy condition to reduce or eliminate food residues and water. For example, do not leave dirty dishes in sink overnight.
❱ Make sure garbage cans have tight-fitting lids.
❱ Use expert advice to maintain suitable pest control programs to prevent their return.

Safety in the kitchen

It is very important to provide a safe environment for children and staff, particularly in the kitchen. Here are some ways to provide a safer environment in the kitchen.

Allow time

▶ Allow yourself enough time for the job. Think carefully about what you are doing. Most accidents happen when you are in a hurry or are not paying attention to what you are doing.

Avoid accidental poisoning

▶ Keep cabinet doors and drawers closed and preferably locked. This will prevent children having access to poisons, cleaners, and dangerous objects. If possible, also store these out of the reach of children.

▶ Avoid storing cleaners and poisons with edible food.

▶ Do not store cleaners and poisons in containers that previously contained foods, such as soft drink bottles.

Beware of physical injury

▶ Make sure drawers have safety catches so they don't crash to the floor when they are pulled out too far.

▶ Never let appliance cords dangle over the counter. If you leave toasters, coffee makers, or other electrical appliances on the counter, unplug them when not in use, place them against the wall, and tuck the cords behind them.

▶ Keep a first aid kit and fire extinguisher handy.

Guard against electrocution

▶ Do not reach into a toaster with a metal utensil unless the toaster is unplugged.

▶ Make sure your hands (and feet) are dry before plugging in or unplugging electrical appliances.

▶ Keep equipment in good repair. Be on the lookout for frayed cords and straining motors.

▶ Explain the danger of electricity to children.

Beware of scalds and burns

▶ Keep items that burn easily (pot holders, towels, or curtains) away from burners and other sources of heat.

▶ When cooking with a covered pan, take the lid off facing away from you to avoid being scalded.

▶ Always supervise children carefully when using hot appliances.

When cooking with children

▶ Before cooking with children, talk with them about safety and rules. Ensure they are aware of potential dangers, such as hot stoves and sharp knives.

▶ Model for children how to cook safely. For example, put your free hand behind your back so you are not tempted to touch the hot pan.

▶ Discuss with older children about how to handle a knife safely. For example, sharp side versus blunt side and keeping fingers out of the way. Children should be shown how to slice with a knife with a backward and forward motion.

▶ Children should not run in the food preparation area.

▶ Children require continuous close supervision with most kitchen utensils and in kitchen areas.

A food safety and hygiene checklist

There are numerous ways to plan, organize, and reflect on your safety and hygiene policies and practices for an early childhood program. Table 4.11 is a checklist that you can use as a planning tool or as a general evaluation-monitoring guide. Create additional items to best meet the purposes and needs of your program.

Table 4.11 A food safety and hygiene checklist

	Yes	No
KITCHEN FACILITIES		
Do you regularly check that the refrigerator is cooling at less than 40°F?		
Do you regularly clean all cooking surfaces such as stoves, ovens, toasters, grills, and microwaves?		
Do you always wipe and then clean with a sanitizer all work surfaces after food preparation is complete?		
Do you regularly clean all food storage areas?		
Do you change all cloth aprons, towels, and dishcloths daily?		
Do you always air dry sanitized utensils and equipment instead of towel drying, if possible?		
Plans needed:		
FOOD HANDLING AND STORAGE		
Do you always wash your hands thoroughly using liquid soap and warm water:		
◗ before, during, and after food preparation?		
◗ before and after wiping tables?		
◗ before setting tables?		
◗ before and after assisting children at meal times?		
Do you avoid preparing or handling food when ill?		
Do you avoid preparing or serving foods if your duties include changing diapers and/or toileting children?		
Do you always discard uneaten portions of food on a plate?		
Do you always use a separate chopping board and equipment for cooked and raw foods?		
Do you reheat food just before serving?		
Do you avoid letting the temperature of hot food fall below 140°F?		
Do you avoid keeping food warm for long periods of time?		
Do you avoid letting cooked food cool down first before placing in the refrigerator?		

Do Carrots Make You See Better?

Table 4.11 *continued*

	Yes	No
Do you thaw all frozen food in the refrigerator or microwave oven?		
Do you always sanitize equipment used for pureeing foods?		
Do you always store food that has been removed from its original packaging in a covered container?		
Do you store raw food below cooked food in the refrigerator?		
Do you always store children's lunches brought from home in a refrigerator or store them in a cool area until eaten?		
Plans needed:		
NURSERY PRACTICES		
Do you always sterilize infant bottles before use and, if possible, after use?		
Do you sterilize all equipment that is needed for preparing the infant formula?		
Do you always check the expiration dates of infant formulas?		
Do you wash the tops of the formula cans before the formula is used?		
Do you always tightly cover and refrigerate formula after it has been prepared?		
Do you always use a formula that has been made from a powdered formula within 24 hours?		
Do you always check the temperature of milk after it has been heated (not in the microwave)?		
Do you always discard partially consumed milk in bottles?		
Do you always remove baby food from jars and serve in dishes for infants?		
Do you always date and store in the refrigerator remaining food in the baby food jar?		
Do you always discard baby food if not eaten within 72 hours of the date it was opened?		
Do you store breast milk in the refrigerator for no more than 48 hours, or in the freezer for no longer than 3 months?		
Do you defrost breast milk in the refrigerator or under cool running water? (It will curdle if put in boiling water.)		
Do you never refreeze or reheat breast milk?		

Table 4.11 *continued*

	Yes	No
Do you ask mothers to supply breast milk in small quantities to prevent waste?		
Plans needed:		
CHILDREN'S FOOD EXPERIENCES		
Hygiene		
Do children wash their hands before eating?		
Do children wash their hands before preparing food?		
Do children avoid handling food unnecessarily when serving?		
Do children share food, cups, plates, or utensils?		
Do you exclude any child who is ill from food activity?		
If using group recipes, is preference given to foods that will be cooked after preparation?		
Plans needed:		
Safety		
Do you explain to children the dangers of hot appliances?		
Do you explain and demonstrate to children the dangers of sharp knives?		
Do you establish rules for use of appliances and equipment?		
Do you wipe up spills at once?		
Do you plan so that electrical cords are not where they can be tripped over?		
Are children expected to sit at tables when eating?		
Are children aware that running in the food preparation area is potentially dangerous?		
Plans needed:		

Section 6

Information and ideas for parents

This section includes several basic food and nutrition topics that may be particularly interesting and useful for both parents and staff. The pages have been formatted so they can be easily copied and circulated. Single copies might be distributed over a period of time, or they could be stapled together to form a reference booklet available in the entrance area of your early childhood center. They can also be modified to be more relevant for individual programs, if required.

Topics addressed are:
- ▶ food foundations for children—some basic nutrition information;
- ▶ food needs—recommendations for menus for child care;
- ▶ snack ideas—for home or while in care;
- ▶ ideas for lunch box or evening meal;
- ▶ facts about vitamins, minerals, and fiber;
- ▶ feeding fussy eaters; and
- ▶ looking after teeth.

Do Carrots Make You See Better?

154

Food foundations for children

What young children eat can significantly affect their future health. Eating habits are formed early in life, so what children eat in their first years can affect what they eat later.

In childhood, eating healthy food assists with the growth and development of young bodies and minds. It also assists with the prevention of illness.

It is important that young children eat a wide variety of food each day so they become familiar with many different foods and are more likely to receive all the nutrients they need for growth and energy. Your child might like to help decide what to eat for breakfast or what to pack for lunch. Foods like fruits, vegetables, bread, cereal, meat or meat alternatives, and dairy products contain many nutrients. However, some foods that children may like, such as chips, candy, and cookies may fill them up, but they contain few nutrients. It is best if children eat these foods only occasionally.

Try to:

• include different nutritious foods each day;

• remember chips, candy, and cookies contain few nutrients; and

• be sure your child has plenty of food for all the time he or she is at the center.

Do Carrots Make You See Better?

Food needs

It is recommended that children get about half their daily nutrient needs while in full day child care. Here is a sample list of food that would meet these requirements. Because these recommendations meet only half the requirements, a similar amount of food needs to be eaten at home (at breakfast and supper). The actual amount eaten will depend on each child's age, appetite, and activity. This is an approximate guide only.

Daily minimum servings for young children in settings 8+ hours

Food	Serve size	Number of servings in care
Breads and cereals (serve a variety)	1 slice bread 1/2 cup cereal 1/3 cup cooked rice 1/2 cup cooked pasta 1 pancake or muffin	2
Fruits and vegetables (try different ones)	1 piece fruit 1/2 cup vegetables 1/2 cup canned fruit	1 fruit, 1 vegetable
Dairy foods (whole fat)	1 cup milk 1 container of yogurt 1 inch square cube cheese 1/2 cup pudding	3
Meat and alternatives	1-1½ oz. (small piece) meat, chicken, or fish 1 egg 1/3 cup legumes	1

A sample menu for an early childhood program

Morning snack	½ cup milk Fruit
Lunch	Baked beans, chicken, ham, tuna or egg sandwich OR Lasagna and salad Vegetable or fruit pieces Water
Afternoon snack	Graham cracker ½ cup milk

Try to:
- **include different nutritious foods each day;**
- **remember chips, candy, and cookies contain few nutrients; and**
- **be sure your child has plenty of food for all the time he or she is at the center.**

Do Carrots Make You See Better?

156

Snack ideas

Fruit and vegetables
- small pieces of fruit;
- slices of fruit;
- frozen fruit pieces: orange segments, sliced banana, grapes, watermelon;
- banana slices coated in coconut;
- dried fruit;
- canned fruit;
- corn on the cob;
- vegetable pieces with dip, such as carrot, celery, broccoli, cauliflower; and
- celery sticks filled with peanut butter or cottage cheese.

Bread and cereals
- rice cakes with peanut butter and honey;
- pancakes;
- muffins;
- waffles;
- raisin bread/toast;
- sandwiches—different types of bread; and
- plain crackers with honey, peanut butter, or cheese.

Dairy foods (whole fat)
- cheese sticks/shapes;
- milk shakes; for example, banana smoothie
- yogurt; and
- dairy desserts.

Drinks
- cool water;
- milk; and
- juice, only occasionally and diluted.

Try to:
- include different nutritious foods each day;
- remember chips, candy, and cookies contain few nutrients; and
- be sure your child has plenty of food for all the time he or she is at the center.

Do Carrots Make You See Better?

Ideas for the lunch box or evening meal

Leftovers
- spaghetti with sauce;
- lasagna;
- casseroles;
- chicken drumsticks; and
- meat, vegetables, and rice.

Salads
- cold meats/chicken/tuna/salmon/ hard-boiled egg;
- different pieces of fruit and vegetables;
- coleslaw; and
- potato/rice/pasta salad.

Others
- muffin pizza;
- spaghetti or baked beans; and
- yogurt/pudding.

Drinks
- cool water;
- milk; and
- juice, diluted (only occasionally).

Sandwiches

Using:
- bread—white/whole wheat/rolls/pita bread;
- crackers; and
- rice cakes.

Try the following filling ideas:
- salad;
- meat/fish/chicken/egg;
- baked beans;
- cheese;
- peanut butter;
- banana;
- cottage cheese mixed with corn or relish;
- carrots and raisins; and
- tuna and mayonnaise.

Fruit and Vegetables
- any sort (cut up or whole).

Try to:
- include different nutritious foods each day;
- remember chips, candy, and cookies contain few nutrients; and
- be sure your child has plenty of food for all the time he or she is at the center.

The USDA Food Pyramid

Vitamins and minerals in the sufficient amounts are essential for good health. If children are seriously lacking in one or more of these, they may not grow and develop to their full potential. The best way to ensure enough nutrients is for children to eat a wide variety of foods and to limit their intake of fatty, sugary, and salty foods. Vitamin and mineral supplements should not be necessary and can lead to health problems if taken in large or incorrect amounts.

Try to:
- include different nutritious foods each day;
- remember chips, candy, and cookies contain few nutrients; and
- be sure your child has plenty of food for all the time he or she is at the center.

The USDA Food Pyramid

Do Carrots Make You See Better?

Feeding fussy eaters

Some young children seem to exist on very little food—some parents would say they live on thin air! They may limit their preferred foods to only a few selections. Children learn very quickly that they can exert power over their parents using food as the focus. Often the tendency to refuse food offered is only short-lived, and if you treat it as a passing phase, it should be just that. If your child is a fussy eater, do not despair. Here are some suggestions that may help.

Try some of these strategies:

▶ do not force the issue;
▶ provide a wide range of food;
▶ consider the presentation of food;
▶ allow children to choose from the food offered;
▶ allow children to serve themselves;
▶ eat the same food with your child;
▶ provide a calm and relaxed environment;
▶ if your child does not eat what is offered, take it away and do not offer anything as a substitute;
▶ remember that the taste of some foods may really not appeal to your child;
▶ often, eating with friends in an early childhood program can encourage a wider variety of food consumption (peer pressure);
▶ do not allow children to fill up on non-nutritious food between meals; and
▶ do not feel guilty if your child will not eat food offered.

Try to:

▶ include different nutritious foods each day;
▶ remember chips, candy, and cookies contain few nutrients; and
▶ be sure your child has plenty of food for all the time he or she is at the center.

Do Carrots Make You See Better?

PHOTOCOPY FOR USE

Looking after teeth

Tooth decay

Your child's teeth are important for appearance, eating, and speaking. Good eating habits begin at an early age.

Children who frequently consume foods containing sugar are at risk for tooth decay. Sugar is found in many children's foods, drinks, and medicines, including syrup medication, teething biscuits, and vitamins.

Teething

Teething can be quite painful for young children. A cold teething ring and mushy food may help. Commercial biscuits may be useful, but homemade biscuits with no salt or sugar, or bread crusts dried in the oven are a better choice.

Cleaning teeth

Teeth should be cleaned as soon as the first tooth erupts by wiping with a clean washcloth or gauze cloth. A small soft toothbrush can be used anytime. Children need an adult to help with toothbrushing until the age of nine to ten years. Children should not swallow large amounts of toothpaste.

Bottle decay and pacifiers

Sugary fluids such as sweetened milk, vitamin syrups, fruit juice drinks, and soft drinks in bottles will increase the risk of tooth decay in babies. Depending on the extent of decay, it can lead to a disturbing appearance, be painful, and may lead to infection through the decayed teeth.

A pacifier dipped in a sweet food, such as honey, can also lead to early tooth decay. Frequent doses of sweet medicines can also cause tooth decay at an early age.

Do not give your child a bottle at bedtime unless absolutely necessary. If you do, be sure to:

- put a child to bed with cool boiled water only;
- do not let a child have a bottle for a long time with a sugary fluid;
- remove the bottle from the child's mouth when asleep; and
- encourage children to drink from a cup as early as possible, at least by 12 months of age.

Try to:

- restrict foods containing sugar, such as sweet drinks and cookies, to meal times and parties;
- avoid giving children sweet snacks between meals; and
- give snacks such as fruit, bread, cheese, vegetable sticks, natural yogurt, and corn on the cob.

Do Carrots Make You See Better?

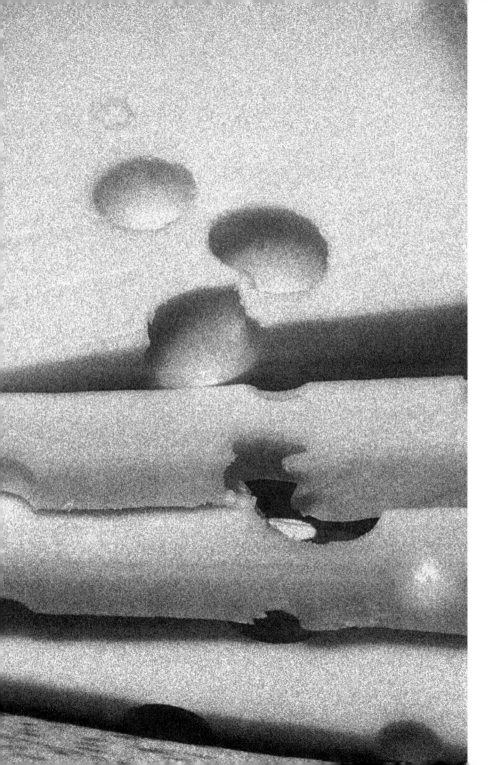

Chapter 5

Making decisions about food foundations

Introduction

There are many issues and challenges surrounding children and their encounters with foods. By considering children's rights, we can bring children, early childhood programs, and food learning together. Early childhood staff and parents can then negotiate relevant and specific standards, policies, and daily practices that will result in the best possible food opportunities for children.

In this chapter, there are six sections containing suggestions, scenarios, challenges, thinking points, ideas, and information. Each section will assist you with making decisions about food foundations and food issues in early childhood programs. The sections are about:
- children's rights from a global perspective;
- strategies for negotiation and mediation if conflicts arise about food issues;
- sample food and nutrition policies to suit different early childhood programs;
- a management process and checklist for planning, organizing, and monitoring food services, education, and other food-related issues;
- further reading about a wide variety of food issues in early childhood programs, including a list of references; and
- a list of organizations that can provide information and resources, which may be useful when deciding about food issues and talking with parents, staff, and children about food and nutrition.

Section 1

Children's rights

Children are especially vulnerable because they are dependent and developing human beings; thus, they need special protection. Rights can be defined as needs, and children's primary needs include the right to food, shelter, and care, health and education, as well as love and affection with understanding and protection from harm. International rights for children were formally established by the United Nations in 1959. The *Declaration of the Rights of the Child* has a preamble and presents the basic rights of children throughout the world as a set of ten principles. For example, Principle One states in part "the child shall enjoy special protection, and shall be given opportunities and facilities...to develop physically, mentally, morally, spiritually and socially in a healthy and normal manner...," and Principle Four includes "...the child shall have the right to adequate nutrition, housing, recreation and medical services."

The *United Nations Convention on the Rights of the Child* is the first formally binding international document to specifically set out the fundamental rights of all children and the obligations of States (nations) to observe those rights. The Convention was adopted by the United Nations' General Assembly in November 1989. The document has a preamble with three major sections that encompass 54 articles. Children's food issues are most directly linked with Articles 3, 24, 28, and 29. As one example, Article 24 outlines the States' broad responsibilities surrounding "the right of the child to enjoyment of the highest attainable standard of health and facilities..." This can happen when measures are taken to provide access to education—"knowledge of child health and nutrition, the advantages of breastfeeding, hygiene and environmental sanitation and the prevention of accidents..."

People's understandings of human rights and the implementation of them vary in both principle and law. Kent (1992) has distinguished the interests of children versus the rights in law of children as soft rights and strong or hard (formal) rights. In a developed country, much of the adult obligation to provide food and food opportunities for children at home and in children's programs lies in the realm of "soft" rights with no legal backing. The provision of high quality and widely varied meals in calm, enjoyable social settings is one ideal but realistic "soft" right. Opportunities within educational programs for children to sensitively explore and comfortably understand food sources and processes are another example of soft rights.

These examples contrast with the very basic provisions of sufficient clean food and water for young children in many developing countries that continue to struggle with drought, famine, and war. However, the United States is not totally exempt from these daily life disasters. There are individuals and specific groups in American society who suffer from poor water sources while others face the dilemma of insufficient money to purchase foods that adequately meet their nutritional needs.

> ## Challenge
>
> Consider the issues raised about children's rights and the relevance of everyday food events in your children's program.

A focus on children's rights and their related needs assists us with setting the scene for discussing the educational principles of supportive environments, social justice, and understanding diversity (see Chapter 2). These principles help shape the ultimate expectations, relationships, and interactions of children and adults that result in either meeting or not meeting children's food-related rights and needs.

In recognizing the importance of children's rights and such principles, many early childhood educators have created ways of accepting and encouraging the diversity of children and families from a wide variety of backgrounds. Publications that are used widely include *Anti-bias Curriculum: Tools for Empowering Young Children* (Derman-Sparks, et al, 1989) and *Valuing Diversity: The Primary Years* (McCracken, 1993).

To some extent, the various types of children's programs will influence what happens when children's rights and these principles are put into daily use. Also, decisions will be influenced by general and specific standards for children's programs. Families and teachers jointly consider and utilize the optional and mandatory standards that seem to best match their particular community and service. The educational standards that you adopt for your personal approach or philosophy to food learning may include standards and/or regulations from an employing body or government department, one or more professional organizations, and a particular philosophical or religious orientation.

Section 2

Negotiating food foundations

The influences of adults' attitudes and actions are considered in this section, and ideas are explored for adults to negotiate agreed-upon actions about food. All of these aspects of food foundations depend on sensitive communication among adults. Many adults have varying beliefs and values—strongly held ideas about personal rights and wrongs, as well as what one does or does not do.

In order for adults to resolve their value differences in the best interests of children, it is vital:

- that program staff have well-developed communication skills;
- that sensible policies are created and shared; and
- that staff and parents routinely resolve any confusions and misunderstandings, varying expectations, or strongly held beliefs.

Relevant standards and documents such as Ethics and the Early Childhood Educator (Laney, 1999) assist adults with balancing various perspectives.

Resolving different perspectives

The idea of resolving differences is often called negotiation. This means that the expectations and practices of various individuals may vary, but each can have equal validity, depending on one's philosophy or perspective. The dilemmas that arise may be minor or major and people's emotional reactions will range from personal discomfort to professional tension or confrontation. In fact, a degree of "conflict" is normal and may be a productive part of people working together (Rodd, 1994). By acknowledging that different perspectives exist, adults can move on to view the "conflict issue" as a challenge, and thus a time for personal or collective growth and change. The purpose of mutual problem solving is to turn conflict into cooperation by finding answers that each person agrees to (Clinard, 1985).

An explicit format and series of questions is provided here. This may help to guide your negotiations about food in early childhood programs.

A negotiator's guide

1. Define goals and objectives
   - Exactly what do I want from this negotiation?
   - What do I have to do to meet my needs?
   - What am I willing to give up to get what I want?
   - What are my time and economic requirements for this negotiation?

2. Clarify the issues
   - What are the issues as I see them?
   - What is the supporting framework for my position?
   - How will I present it to the other party?
   - What are the issues as seen by the other party?
   - How will they support their position?
   - What appear to be the significant differences in the way the parties view the issues?

3. Gather information
   - Who will I be negotiating with and what do I know about them? How do they approach a negotiation? What are their ego needs?

- When and where will the negotiation take place? What advantages or disadvantages do the alternatives have for me? ... for the other party?
- What are the economic, political, and human implications of the issues?
- What personal power do I have that can be used constructively in this negotiation?

4. Humanize and set the climate; prepare for conflict
- How can I best establish rapport with the other party?
- How can I establish a win/win climate?
- What will be the major points of conflict?
- How will I determine what the other party needs as compared to what they want?

5. Compromise/resolution of the issues
- How will I attempt to resolve conflict? How will I respond to the other party's attempts to resolve conflict?
- Will I involve a third, neutral party to mediate the areas of conflict between the parties?
- What concessions am I prepared to make? Under what conditions?
- What do I expect in return for my concessions?

6. Agreement and confirmation
- How formal must it be?
- What approval process will be required? How long will it take?
- What implementation steps will be needed?

(*Source:* Adapted from Maddux, R. (1988). *Successful Negotiation.* Los Altos: Crisp Pubs, Inc. pp 57–58.)

An early childhood example

Following is a relevant example of how one child care center addressed a potentially divisive food issue by negotiation. The following letter was drafted by the management committee after consultation with staff and parents.

Late snack

Dear Parents,

Concerns have been raised about the snack that children bring from home to eat at approximately 4:30 pm. As a result, we are reviewing the late snack and seek your views before making a decision about this.

The concerns raised are:
- The large number of junk food items being sent for children such as chocolate, softdrinks, and chips.
- The amount of waste. Often large snacks are thrown out.
- Complaints that evening meals are not eaten as children are not hungry.
- Occasionally the late snack is seen as an adequate substitute for the evening meal with "meal" type snacks being sent. This causes concern over appropriate eating patterns and adequate nutrition for children.
- Late snack has turned into a "best snack" competition for some children, leading others to lose interest in their "plain" food.

The need for children to have a late snack has also been questioned. In this center, provided meals are always nutritious and tasty, as well as in sufficient quantity to suit all appetites.

Please complete the following survey.

Thank you

Late snack survey

Please check your preferred options and add comments

1) delete snack time and make afternoon snack (2:45—3:00 pm) later, with a drink of milk at about 4:30 pm;   ☐

2) delete snack time and make afternoon snack later, with a drink of "juice" provided by parents;   ☐

3) leave late afternoon snack as is, but stipulate snacks are to be only a piece of fruit or a sandwich with juice, milk, or water to drink.   ☐

4) Your comments:_____

_____

_____

_____

_____

_____

The following letter was then circulated to all parents.

Late snack survey results

Dear Parents,

The result of our survey indicates that the late snack will be replaced by a drink of milk or soy milk as of this week. The survey results were:

Total responses: 21

1) delete snack time and replace with a drink of milk: 12

2) delete snack time and replace with own drink: 2

3) leave snack as is: 5

4) don't mind/other suggestions: 2

We have sought guidance from a nutritionist familiar with USDA nutrition regulations. Children aged 2–5 yrs need approximately 2–3 snacks as well as 3 regular, nutritionally balanced meals. I have discussed with the nutritionist our concerns about late snack and have relayed details of the concerns expressed at parent meetings and by individual parents. She fully supports the idea of giving a glass of milk to the children at approximately 4:30 pm and considers milk to be a "food drink." At her suggestion, we will provide soy milk for children who are unable to tolerate cow's milk.

If parents have any concerns about this issue, please see me to discuss how these may be addressed. Thank you

The Director

LATE SNACK

As of Monday, you will no longer have to pack a late snack for your child. We will be providing children with a drink of milk or soy milk (for children who cannot drink cow's milk).

Thank you

After further discussion seeking feedback, this notice was displayed prominently in the center.

Attitudes and actions related to food events

Prior to writing this book, staff working in a variety of children's programs were asked to identify important attitudes, roles, and responsibilities surrounding food foundations. Many examples were provided. These have been reviewed and clustered together for consideration as you identify and negotiate food practices, or as you implement and evaluate food events. Some important issues were:

- adults, both parents and staff, are accountable for children's future health, and their growth and development;
- adults should value everyday experiences such as cooking as learning, not only numbers and ABCs;
- there is conflict between adults' rights to choose food and then being role models for children when eating—this applies to parents and staff;
- children require appropriate relaxed settings while eating;
- it is important to involve children in choices and decisions about foods, including preparation and clean-up;
- staff should respect parents' wishes with regard to foods;
- good communication between parents and staff is essential for good relationships, mutual understanding, and respect;
- it is important to provide sufficient choice for differing tastes;
- there is value in talking about media advertising of food and body image messages; and
- allowing children to decide when they have eaten enough is essential practice.

There will be important issues that are specific for your program and community. You can add them to this list.

_____

_____

_____

_____

Challenge

Use this list of beliefs and practices as scenarios that educators and parents can share and discuss at staff meetings, during parent meetings, or when evaluating your program. Explore the enablers and barriers of each scenario. In terms of using these ideas for staff learning and growth, we believe that the wider community should be supportive of early childhood staff and assist by providing facilities for staff development.

Negotiating perspectives and practices

A number of activities are presented below for staff and parents to share and review during staff meetings, staff development sessions, or parent meetings.

1. What is right? Discuss the following situation, considering what is right rather than what is expedient: Several three- to five-year-old children are lined up against a wall, given food one by one, and told, "No talking; eat your food."

2. Sitting in their chair at the table. The phrase "How would you feel if ..." provides a task that challenges adults to view various food opportunities from a child's point of view. For example, how would you feel if someone was hovering over you while you were eating, constantly pressuring or nagging, telling you to hurry and finish? Here is a second example: Sitting on the floor at snack time, a three-year-old spilled his milk when bumped by another child. The caregiver yelled at him and said he was stupid and careless (McCrea, 1988).

Challenge

For each example above, talk about the roles and perspectives of being a teacher and a child. Do this by:
- describing the incident from the child's point of view;
- describing the incident from the staff member's and/or parent's point of view; and
- discussing the disparity between these points of view.

Draw on your knowledge of human development and early childhood programs, as well as examples from working with children and other adults. Seriously consider if adults would do these things to each other; if not, why act this way with children?

Thinking points

Trusting children is a key component of quality children's programs. However, it is also something that is more often advocated than achieved.

In your early childhood program, what aspects could be adapted to be more respectful of children's capabilities?

Section 3

Sample food education and nutrition policies

Following are some sample policies. Remember these are examples only and policies need to be developed and adapted for each individual program to suit its own particular needs. Each program is encouraged to review the general policy closest to their needs and use it as a basis for developing a policy to suit the individual characteristics of their own program.

There are many resources available to assist staff and parents with understanding and developing policies, including *Model child care health policies*, NAEYC (1993).

It is important to formalize food and nutrition practices with a written food and nutrition policy. This can be a separate policy or a part of the overall policy of the program.

Policies should be developed with reference to the general philosophy of the center and the identified needs of the children. Also, broader factors such as government regulations, should be taken into account.

A suggested procedure for developing a food and nutrition policy is as follows:
- meet with parents and staff to discuss the need for a policy and the major issues to be addressed;
- form a sub-committee to develop the policy;
- collect information and resources and seek assistance if necessary;
- draft policies;
- refer to parents and staff for comment and/or adjustment;
- ratify policies with staff, parents, and the management committee of the program;
- agree upon an evaluation process; and
- review policies after a specified period, perhaps on a yearly basis.

Policy for food living and food learning

SAMPLE

Aim

This program is designed to assist children in gradually understanding their own personal health requirements and physical needs. We aim to recognize and facilitate each child's nutritional needs and encourage both the children and parents to develop a good food sense. Through suitable food experiences, all of the child's developmental areas (social, emotional, cultural, cognitive, language, spiritual, physical, and so on) are enhanced.

Explanation

Food living

The program recognizes that within the group, children have different nutritional needs, including allergies and illnesses. In order to develop to their fullest potential, children need a well-balanced, varied diet, and we encourage parents to be aware of this. Teachers will work with parents to provide a variety of foods suitable for their children. All staff will be positive role models by practicing appropriate food-related behavior.

Food learning

"During the early childhood years, children form habits and attitudes that can last a lifetime" (Kendrick et al, 1995). Parents and teachers will work as partners in children's food and nutrition education. Teachers will provide learning experiences for children that enhance the development of good eating habits. Children will learn about foods and meal expectations during the early childhood years.

Implementation

We ask parents to assist us in providing and meeting the following food-related experiences for the children.

Food living

- Meals will happen in a social setting where the whole group meets together; sometimes individual and small group opportunities are valuable and appropriate.
- Meal times will promote healthy food-related habits and sufficient space will be allocated in calm settings.
- Adults will interact with children during meal times and provide a model of healthy food-related habits.

- Parents will be involved in planning and implementing children's menus.
- Staff will be sensitive to any special dietary needs of individual children.
- Children will wash their hands before and after eating.
- As we strive for better health and nutrition in our program, we suggest and prefer that parents not send pre-packaged or processed foods for morning/afternoon snacks.
- For morning and afternoon snacks, children should be provided with fresh fruit, raw vegetables, crackers, or yogurt, rather than chocolates, cookies, cakes, or candy.
- For lunch, children will be provided with sandwiches or simple dishes.
- Water will always be available for children.
- For birthdays, arrangements need to be made with the teacher(s) about special cakes being brought in. (We encourage healthier-style cakes and other "party" options for varied experiences).

Food learning

- Teachers will provide parents with information via pamphlets, regular newsletters, and the bulletin board about the importance of balanced and varied meals.
- Through hands-on food experiences, children will create, explore the environment, learn problem solving, and personal interaction skills and be exposed to foods from other cultures.

Source: Developed by N. McCrea with early childhood teaching students, QUT. Format from *Keeping on Track* (1988) Community Child Care Co-operative, NSW. This sample policy statement provides a reasoned position, a rationale, and several daily practices.

Infant and toddler nutrition policy

Child care center

SAMPLE

This center is committed to ensuring that:

▶ Food and drinks meet children's daily nutritional requirements and are culturally appropriate.

▶ Meal times promote healthy nutritional habits.

▶ Food is prepared and stored hygienically.

In order to meet these aims, the following policy is designed for the nursery unit.

Breast milk/Formula

▶ Breast feeding mothers will be supported and a comfortable area for this will be available.

▶ Bottles of milk (formula or expressed breast milk) must be clearly labeled with the infant's name and date and must be stored in the kitchen refrigerator.

▶ Parents should provide adequate milk for the child's attendance.

▶ If infants are given expressed breast milk, encourage cups or straw cups. It is easier for an infant to suck on a nipple of a bottle, and this may discourage him or her from accepting the breast after getting used to the bottle.

▶ Formula/expressed breast milk needs to be heated only to room temperature or slightly warmer, according to the infant's preference. Do not heat more than once. Parents are encouraged to provide more bottles with smaller amounts of milk to aid this.

▶ When necessary, proper sterilization procedures are followed for bottles, nipples, and other utensils used for very young infants.

Introduction of solids

▶ Breast milk or formula meet all the infant's nutritional requirements until the age of six months.

▶ Solids should be introduced between four to six months of age, initially to introduce the infant to different textures and tastes and colors. Parents should be consulted regarding the introduction of solids.

▶ As breast milk or formula is the major source of nutrients, when solids are first introduced, they should be given after a milk feed.

▶ We recognize the immaturity of the infant's digestive and renal (kidney) system, so solids should be introduced one at a time in small amounts. This enables the caregiver to identify reactions to particular foods.

Do Carrots Make You See Better?

Examples of reactions include rashes, unusual bowel movements, and vomiting. The director and parents are informed of such reactions.

▶ Suggested first solids:
  — rice cereal
  — pureed vegetables, such as pumpkin
  — pureed cooked fruit, such as apple and pear
  — mashed ripe banana or avocado

  ▶ Rice cereal and pureed cooked fruit is available for infants who are being introduced to solids.

▶ After being established on solids, foods that are mashed or chopped can be introduced under supervision. This encourages the infant to develop the foundations of chewing skills. Harder foods, such as biscuits, are introduced under close supervision (to guard against choking). Other food given to the older children will be sent from the kitchen (see menu guide). Highly spiced foods will be avoided.

▶ We acknowledge that after six months of age, solids start to become major sources of nutrients and calories. Iron stores in the infant are now depleted, so it is important to introduce iron-rich foods such as meat, liver, chicken, and fish that is cooked and pureed.

▶ Foods offered to infants will not contain any added salt, sugar, or fat.

▶ Parents will indicate on the enrollment form any known allergies or food reactions. Foods that are most likely to cause allergic reactions are cow's milk, egg white, and wheat, so the introduction of these foods should be delayed, especially in infants with family histories of food allergies.

▶ Cow's milk should not be introduced as a drink for infants under 12 months of age. Custards or yogurt can be introduced around six to eight months of age.

▶ Cooked egg yolk can be introduced around six to eight months of age, while cooked egg white can be introduced around 10–12 months of age.

▶ Diets different to this policy will be accommodated when possible at the director's/nurse's discretion with a signed doctor's authorization.

▶ Families providing food from home are expected to follow the center's Nutrition Policy while the child is in attendance at the center. Just as staff cannot give medicine to a child outside of the center's policy, foods outside of the policy will not be given.

▶ Special occasion (birthday, holiday) foods will be limited and parents notified of any change to the child's diet.

▶ Staff will not force infants to eat foods. Even at a young age, the child's choice will be respected. Food will not be used as a bribe or punishment.

▶ Appropriate seating and sized utensils will be used for young infants in a pleasant eating environment.

▶ Any concerns with this policy should be directed to the director.

Source: Developed by Galbiri Child Care and Preschool Centre Incorporated, Townsville, Qld.

Preschool nutrition policy

Child care center

SAMPLE

Goal

To provide children in full-day child care with at least 50% of their daily recommended dietary intake of nutrients in the form of safe and appetizing foods.

Strategies

- Milk will be served with morning snack.
- All dairy products will be whole fat.
- Only soy milks that are fortified with calcium will be used as substitutes for cow's milk.
- Water will be available at all times.
- Children are allowed to have second helpings of fruit or milk-based desserts.
- Parents will be advised when their child is not eating well.
- When children are on special diets the parents will be asked to provide the cook with as much detail as possible about suitable foods.
- Gloves will be worn or food tongs used by any staff directly handling cooked foods.
- Children will wash their hands before handling food or eating meals and snacks.
- Food will be stored and served at safe temperatures.
- If children are still hungry after the first serving, they may have a second helping of food.

Goal

To provide an eating environment that assists the transmission of family and multicultural values.

Strategies

- Food will not be used as a form of punishment either by its provision or denial.
- Recipes and food awareness activities will be chosen from a variety of cultures.
- Special occasions may be celebrated with culturally appropriate foods.
- Parents will be invited to at least one food occasion each year.
- Recipes for food served in the center will be available to parents.
- The weekly menu will be on display for parents.

Goal

To teach children about food and nutrition.

Strategies

- Food awareness activities will be included in the teaching curriculum.
- Children will be encouraged to get hands-on experience in food preparation.
- The foods being served to children will be discussed with them.
- Heights and weights of children will be measured as an activity to demonstrate physical growth.

Source: Developed by Galbiri, Child Care and Preschool Centre Incorporated, Townsville, Qld and modeled on policy sample in *Caring for Children* by Bunney and Williams.

Nutrition policy

When food is brought from home

SAMPLE

Goal

To supervise and assist in children receiving a safe and nutritious diet.

Strategies

- Parents will receive advice on both suitable and unsuitable food to pack for their children.
- Fruit juice will be diluted with water (50/50).
- Water will be available at all times.
- All dairy products provided by the center will be whole fat.
- Emergency food will always be available for children who have brought insufficient food.
- Children will have access to breads/cereals or fruits/vegetable snacks if they are hungry between meals.
- Parents will be advised when their child is not eating well.
- Children will wash their hands before handling food or eating meals and snacks.
- Food will be stored and served at safe temperatures.

Goal

To provide an eating environment that assists the transmission of family and multicultural values.

Strategies

- Staff members will sit with children at mealtime.
- Food is never to be used as a form of punishment either by its provision or denial.
- Multicultural differences will be recognized and accepted.
- Food awareness activities will be chosen from a variety of cultures.
- Special occasions may be celebrated with culturally appropriate foods.
- Parents will be invited to at least one food occasion each year.

Goal

To teach children about food and nutrition.

Strategies

- Food awareness activities will be included in the center program.
- Children will be encouraged to get practical experience in food preparation.
- The foods being eaten by the children will be discussed with them.

Source: Caring for Children by Bunney and Williams (1996).

After and before school nutrition policy

SAMPLE

Nutrition

- Morning snack and afternoon snack will be provided when appropriate and a suitable break will be arranged to allow for lunch.
- Staff should supervise all meal breaks to ensure that children are receiving sustenance and fluids during the day.
- Staff should encourage children to be seated while eating and drinking.
- If a child does not have lunch during school holidays, the program will supply a balanced meal for the child, the cost of which will be added to the parents' account.
- Programs should supply healthy balanced meals to meet the dietary needs of the children.

Food preparation

- All programs should have a clean and hygienic area for food preparation, with hot and cold running water.
- Children will not be in the cooking area unsupervised while cooking is in progress.
- All staff and children involved in food preparation should wash hands prior to the activity.
- No animals should be in this area.
- Consideration should always be given to special dietary needs of children.

Source: Queensland Children's Activity Network, QCAN.

Do Carrots Make You See Better?

Family child care nutrition policy

A healthy balance of food and drink in sufficient quantity is required on a daily basis. If the provider is providing the food, care should be taken to avoid allergy-inducing food and drink (in children with known conditions) and consideration should be given to dietary, cultural, and religious preferences.

Procedures

▶ Parents and care providers should communicate about a child's routine and food requirements.

▶ Some foods, such as whole nuts, are inappropriate for small children. Extra care should be taken with food for babies and toddlers—a sensible practice is to grate the more solid fruits and vegetables, and cut softer foods into bite-sized pieces of "finger" foods to ensure that they are easily swallowed.

▶ Liquids, including milk, water, and fruit juice should be offered regularly throughout the day and frequently during summer.

▶ Plenty of fresh food in the form of fruit and vegetables needs to be offered, especially for morning and afternoon snack or whenever a quick snack is needed. An occasional sweet treat may be provided for variety and special occasions.

▶ Children are encouraged to be seated for a meal, as this is much more convivial for sharing as a group, and children are more likely to chew and digest their food properly.

Source: Lady Gowrie Child Centre Family Day Care, Paddington Qld.

Do Carrots Make You See Better?

Section 4

A management process for food issues in early childhood services

A self-study guide for managing food issues is outlined in Table 5.1 for use in various early childhood settings. It can be an initial planning establishment guide, an ongoing planning cycle tool, or a more formal appraisal checklist.

It is a quick and simple tool, yet allows for in-depth planning, monitoring, and documenting of the food-related activities in children's programs. Issues included in the guide are food-related philosophy, policies, goals, roles of staff and parents, and educational needs of children and adults.

Table 5.1 A self-study guide for food issues (This table is adapted from McCrea, 1986.)

Management Process	Yes	Could be better	No	Who will do it? When will it happen? When will it be reviewed?
1. Have you included food issues in the philosophy of your early childhood program? Have you: ▶ met with staff, parents, and relevant community members to decide on food issues; ▶ considered topics such as diversity, social justice, and supportive environments; ▶ discussed the various ways that children learn; and ▶ considered all dimensions of health?				
2. Have you developed appropriate food and nutrition policies that consider: ▶ relevant regulations; ▶ the philosophy of your program; ▶ establishment of operating procedures; and ▶ food and nutrition goals and objectives; 　—for food service; 　—for food learning? (Refer to the previous section with sample food and nutrition policies.)				

Do Carrots Make You See Better?

Table 5.1 *continued*

Management Process	Yes	Could be better	No	Who will do it? When will it happen? When will it be reviewed?
3. Does a single person have overall responsibility for food issues and receiving input from: ▶ the food preparation person (cook); ▶ parents; ▶ teacher; ▶ children; and ▶ consultants?				
4. Have you planned and implemented child-centered food experiences and eating times, taking into account: ▶ relevance to children's interests, needs, skills, and stage of development; ▶ appropriateness of various learning approaches (for example, decision-making, emergent curriculum); ▶ opportunities to transfer learning to various contexts; ▶ individual, family, and cultural needs; ▶ the importance of mealtimes being a social event; and ▶ the space, time, and human resources available?				
5. Have the roles for your food preparation person been defined including: ▶ a clearly written job description; ▶ a detailed roster of duties; ▶ responsibilities to be shared with other staff; and ▶ ongoing training?				

Do Carrots Make You See Better?

Table 5.1 *continued*

Management Process	Yes	Could be better	No	Who will do it? When will it happen? When will it be reviewed?
6. Has the staff's involvement with foods been defined, considering: ▶ when and what foods to prepare; ▶ when and what to clean up; ▶ whether food activities should be held in the kitchen and/or classroom; ▶ attitudes and approaches to adopt during meals and other food-related activities; ▶ physical arrangements for meals and learning; and ▶ consideration of hygiene and safety issues.				
7. Has the role of parents and volunteers in food learning activities been considered with respect to: ▶ planning activities; ▶ implementation—working with children; and ▶ review—feedback and ideas for improvement?				
8. Are there opportunities for parents and staff to broaden their knowledge about early childhood food issues, covering topics such as: ▶ nutritional requirements; ▶ influence of advertising; ▶ food learning opportunities; and ▶ safety and food hygiene.				
9. Evaluation—outline your plans for reflecting, replanning, and being accountable.				
10. Are there any other food issues relevant to you and your program? Define, describe, and discuss these.				

Do Carrots Make You See Better?

Section 5

References and resources

This section contains references used in the preparation of this book and resources for further reading.

Chapter 1 – An introduction to food foundations

References

Birch, L., Johnson, S., and Fisher, J. (1995). Children's eating: The development of food-acceptance patterns. *Young Children*, 50(2), 71-78.

Jones, E. and Nimmo, J. (1994). *Emergent curriculum*. Washington, DC: NAEYC.

Katz, L. and Chard, S. (2000). *Engaging children's minds: The project approach* (2nd ed.). Westport, CT: Ablex.

Reynolds, J. and Dommer, E. (1995). Translating a theoretical framework for food and nutrition education into classroom action. *Journal of the Home Economics Institute of Australia,* 2(4), 7-12.

Further reading

Berk, L. and Winsler, A. (1995). *Scaffolding children's learning: Vygotsky and early childhood education*. Washington, DC: NAEYC.

Edwards, C., Gandini, L., and Forman, G. (eds.). (1998). *The hundred languages of children: The Reggio Emilia approach—Advanced reflections*. Westport, CT: Ablex.

Workman, S. and Anziano, M. (1993). Curriculum webs: Weaving connections from children to teachers. *Young Children*, 48(2), 4-9.

Chapter 2 – A framework for learning about food

References

Appleton, J., Giskes, K., and Patterson, C. (1999). Health Promotion and Food Practice in Early Childhood Services. Program and Abstracts. 11th National Health Promotion Conference, Perth, Western Australia.

Bredekamp, S. (ed.). (1997). *Developmentally appropriate practice in early childhood programs serving children from birth through age 8*. Washington, DC: NAEYC.

Reynolds, J., Dommers, E., and Spillman, D. (1994). Towards a framework for school-based food and nutrition education. *Journal of the Home Economics Institute of Australia*, 1(4), 19-32.

World Health Organization. (1986). *The Ottawa Charter for Health Promotion*. World Health Organization, Geneva.

Further reading

Derman-Sparks, L. and the ABC Task Force. (1989). *Anti-bias curriculum: Tools for empowering young children*. Washington, DC: NAEYC.

National Academy of Early Childhood Programs. (1991). *Accreditation criteria and procedures* (rev. edn). Washington, DC: NAEYC.

Chapter 3 – Approaches to children's learning

References

Berman, C. and Fromer, J. (1991). *Teaching children about food: A teaching and activities guide*. Palo Alto, CA: Bull Pub Co.

Bodrova, E. and Leong, D. (1995). *Tools of the mind: The Vygotskian approach to early childhood education*. Paramus, NJ: Prentice Hall.

Bromley, K. (1995). *Webbing with literature: Creating story maps with children's books*. (2nd edn). Boston: Allyn and Bacon.

Fraser, R. (1994). *Food and nutrition education for 2- to 5-year-olds*. Unpub. BEd. project. Brisbane: QUT.

Knight, T. (1993). Health Development Foundation. (1993). *Earthworks: An adventure in gardening for teachers and children*. South Melbourne: MacMillan Education Australia Pty Ltd.

McCrea, N. (1996). Being sustainable gardeners and wise consumers from an early age. *Educating Young Children*, 2(4), 10-12.

Queensland School Curriculum Council. (1998). *Preschool curriculum guidelines*. Brisbaner: QSCC.

Reynolds, J., Dommers, E., and Spillman, D. (1994). Towards a framework for school-based foods and nutrition education. *Journal of the Home Economics Institutes of Australia*, 1(4), 19-32.

Veitch, B. and Harms, T. (1995). *Learning from cooking experiences: A teacher's guide to accompany COOK AND LEARN*. Menlo Park: Addison-Wesley Pub Co.

Whaley, K. and Swader, E.B. (1990). Multicultural education in infant and toddler settings. *Childhood Education*, 66(4), 238-240.

Wilson, J. and Hoyne, P. (1991). *Cooking with class: Celebrating festivals and cooking*. South Melbourne: Oxford University Press.

Workman, S. and Anziano, M. (1993). Curriculum webs: Weaving connections from children to teacher. *Young Children*, 48(2), 4-9.

Further reading

Approach 1—Decision-making

Hendrick, J. (1997). *Total learning: Developmental curriculum for the young child*. Upper Saddle River, NJ: Prentice Hall.

Hole, E. (1988). Caregiver's corner snack time as a choosing time. *Young Children*, September, 40.

Approach 2—Science and mathematics

D'Amico, J. and Drummond, K. (1994). *The science chef: 100 fun food experiments and recipes for kids*. New York: Wiley.

Harlan, J. and Rivkin, M. (1992). *Science experiences for the early childhood years*. Upper Saddle River, NJ: Prentice Hall.

Holt, B. (1999). *Science with young children*. Washington, DC: NAEYC.

Mandell, M. (1994). *Simple kitchen experiments: Learning science with everyday foods*. New York: Sterling Publishing Co. Inc.

Nailon, D. (1996). Creating optimum environments for infants and toddlers. *Educating Young Children*, 2(4), 13-15.

Approach 3 – Food cycles

Ocone, L. and Pranis, E. (1990). *Kids gardening: A complete guide for teachers, parents and youth leaders*. The National Gardening Association. New York: Wylie Science Editions.

Approach 4 – Language, drama and social studies

List of children's picture books

Ashley, B. (1995). *Cleversticks*. New York: Random House.

Brett, J. (1996). *Goldilocks and the three bears*. New York: Putnam.

Carle, E. (1984). *The very hungry caterpillar*. New York: Putnam.

dePaola, T. (1992). *Jamie O'Rourke and the big potato*. New York: Putnam.

dePaola, T. (1989). *Strega Nona*. New York: Simon and Schuster.

Ehlert, L. (1991). *Growing vegetable soup*. San Diego: Harcourt Brace.

Fox, M. (1990). *Possum magic*. San Diego: Harcourt Brace.

Galdone, P. (1985). *The little red hen*. New York: Houghton Mifflin.

Krauss, R. (1993). *The carrot seed*. New York: Harper Collins.

Lottridge, C.B. (1990). *One watermelon seed*. UK: Oxford University Press.

Rowe, J. (1990). *Scallywag*. New York: Scholastic.

Vaughan, M.K. (1995). *Wombat stew*. New York: Scholastic.

Vernon Lord, J. (1987). *The giant jam sandwich*. New York: Houghton Mifflin.

Zamorano, A. (1997). *Let's eat!* New York: Scholastic.

Cultures

Derman-Sparks, L. (1989). *The anti-bias curriculum*. Washington, DC: NAEYC.

Mallory, B. and New, R. (eds.). (1994). *Diversity and developmental appropriate practices*. New York: Teachers College Press.

Veitch, B. and Harms, T. (1981). *Cook and Learn: Pictorial single portion recipes: A child's cook book*. Reading, MA: Addison Wesley.

Approach 5 – Physical activities and motor skills

Bredekamp, S. (ed.). (1997). *Developmentally appropriate practice in early childhood programs serving children from birth through age 8*. Washington, DC: NAEYC.

Ferreira, N. (1982). *Learning through cooking: A cooking program for children two to ten*. Palo Alto, CA: R and E Research Associates.

Flack, M. and Wiese, R. (1983). *The story about Ping*. New York: Viking.

Mahy, M. (1990). *The seven chinese brothers*. New York: Scholastic.

Veitch, B. and Harms, T. (1981). *Learning from cooking experiences: A teacher's guide to accompany COOK AND LEARN*. Menlo Park: Addison-Wesley.

Approach 6 – Food selection, preparation and presentation

Ferreira, N. (1982). *Learning through cooking: A cooking program for children two to ten*. Palo Alto, CA: R and E Research Associates.

Goodwin, M. and Pollan, G. (1990). *Creative food experiences for children*. Washington, DC: Center for Science in the Public Interest.

Mollie, K. and Henderson, A. (1994). *Pretend soup and other real recipes*. Berkeley, CA: Tricycle Press.

Veitch, B. and Harms, T. (1981). *Cook and learn: Pictorial single portion recipes: A child's cook book*. Menlo Park: Addison-Wesley.

Wilson, J. and Hoyne, P. (1991*). Cooking with class: Celebrating festivals with cooking*. South Melbourne: Oxford University Press.

Chapter 4 – Food and nutrition issues and information

References

Australian Nutrition Foundation. (1995). *Food and Nutrition Accreditation Guidelines for Child Care Centres*. Queensland Branch: ANF.

DeVries, S., Harris, V., McCrea, N., and Danby, S. (1998). Breast-feeding and child care. *Child Care and Children's Health*. A Parent Information Binder, Melbourne, Vic: Centre for Community Child Health and Ambulatory Pediatrics, Royal Children's Hosp.

McCrea, N. (1995). Summertime…and the living is easy. *Every Child*, 30(6), 23.

Public Health Association of Australia. (1995). *Breastfeeding statement*. Adopted at AGM of PHA.

Further reading

Section 2 – Nutritional needs of infants and young children.

Enders, J.B. and Rockwell, R. (1994). *Food, nutrition and the young child*. New York: MacMillan Publishing Company.

Section 3 – Children with special food needs

Meyer, E. (1997). *Feeding your allergic child*. New York: St. Martin's Press.

Section 4 – Meal planning

Berman, C. and Fromer, J. (1997). *Meals without squeals*. Palo Alto, CA: Bull Pub. Co.

Wilson, J. and Hoyne, P. (1991). *Cooking with class: Celebrating festivals with cooking*. South Melbourne: Oxford University Press.

Section 5 – Safety and food hygiene

Kendrick, A.S., Kaufmann R., and Messenger, K.P. (1995). *Healthy young children: A manual for programs*. Washington, DC: NAEYC.

Marotz, L.R., Cross, M.Z., and Rush, J.M. (1993). *Health, safety and nutrition for the young child*. Albany: Delmar Publishers Inc.

Section 6 – Information and ideas for parents

Johnson, S. (1989). When is dessert not dessert? *Young Children*, July, 66.

Lappe, F.M. (1991). *Diet for a small planet*. (20th anniversary edition). New York: Ballantine.

Satter, E. (2000). *Child of mine: Feeding with love and good sense*. Palo Alto, CA: Bull Pub. Co.

Satter, E. (1987). *How to get your kid to eat… But not too much*. Palo Alto, CA: Bull Pub. Co.

Chapter 5 – Making decisions about food foundations

References

Clinard, H.H. (1985). *Winning ways to succeed with people*. Houston: Gulf Publishing Company.

Derman-Sparks, L. and the ABC Task Force. (1989). *Anti-bias curriculum: Tools for empowering young children*. Washington, DC: NAEYC.

Feeney, S. (1999). *Ethics and the early childhood educator: Using the NAEYC code*. Washington, DC: NAEYC.

Kendrick, A.S., Kaufmann, R., and Messenger, K.P. (1995). *Healthy young children: A manual for programs*. Washington, DC: NAEYC.

Kent, G. (1992). *Children's rights to adequate nutrition*. An unpublished document from the International Nutrition Conference. Political Science, University of Hawaii.

McCracken, J.B. (1993). *Valuing diversity: The primary years*. Washington, DC: NAEYC.

McCrea, N. (1986). *Nutrition: a quality component of early childhood.* Proceedings of AAECE's National Open Conference, Hill, T. (ed.)., Adelaide, SA. pp 76-81.

Stonehouse, A. (1991). *Opening the doors: Child care in a multicultural society.* Watson, ACT: AECA. (There is a supporting video, "Tumbalong.")

Stonehouse, A. (1991). *Our code of ethics at work.* AECA Resource Booklet No. 2. Watson, ACT: AECA.

Thody, A. (1993). *Developing your career in education management.* London: Longman.

Further reading

Section 1 – Children's rights

New, R. (1990). Excellent early education: A city in Italy has it. *Young Children*, 45(6), 4-10.

World Health Organization. (1986) *Ottawa Charter for Health Promotion.* Copenhagen: WHO.

Section 2 - Negotiating food foundations

Maddux, R. (1988). *Successful negotiation.* Los Altos, CA: Crisp Pubs. Inc.

Patterson, C., Fleet, A., and Duffie, J. (1995). *Learning from stories: Early childhood professional experiences.* Sydney: Harcourt Brace.

Rodd, J. (1994). *Leadership in early childhood: The pathway to professionalism.* Melbourne: Allen and Unwin.

Stonehouse, A. (1981). *Ourselves in their shoes.* Melbourne: Lady Gowrie Childcare Center.

Section 3 – Sample food education and nutrition policies

Aronson, S., Smith, H., and Martin, J. (1997). *Model child care health policies* (3rd ed). Washington, DC: NAEYC (includes a computer disc with policies).

National Association for the Education of Young Children. (1993). *Model child care health policies.* Washington, DC: NAEYC.

Schwartz, N. (1991). Position paper on nutrition in child care settings. *Journal of Nutrition Education*, 23, 49-50.

Section 4 – A management process for food issues in early childhood programs

Bredekamp, S. (ed.). (1987). *Accreditation criteria and procedures.* Washington, DC: NAEYC.

Multicultural references

Derman-Sparks, L. and the ABC Task Force. (1989). *Anti-bias curriculum: Tools for empowering young children.* Washington, DC: NAEYC.

Soto, L. (1991). Understanding bilingual/bicultural young children. *Young Children*, 46(2), 30-36.

Stonehouse, A. (1991). *Opening the doors.* Watson: AECA.

Whaley, K. and Swadner, E. (1990). Multicultural education in infant and toddler settings. *Childhood Education*, 66(4), 238-240.

Wilson, J. and Hoyne, P. (1991). *Cooking with class: Celebrating festivals with cooking.* South Melbourne: Oxford University Press.

Wood, B. (ed.). (1977). *Tucker in Australia.* Melbourne: Hill of Content.

Section 6

Organizations for resources and information

This is a list of organizations that may be useful when talking with parents, teachers, and children about food and nutrition. Some have lists of resources that can be ordered by contacting the organization. To obtain resources for specific foods, select the food item (wheat, rice, apples, and so on) and locate the relevant resource in your area or check out the United States Department of Agriculture's web site:www.usda.gov.

National organizations and companies

(Please note: At press time these contact details were correct, but they are subject to change. Your local telephone book would be a good starting point for finding out about changes.)

American Diabetes Association, National Office
1701 N. Beauregard St.
Alexandria, VA 22311
800-342-2383
www.diabetes.org/ada/info.asp

American Egg Board
1460 Renaissance Drive
Park Ridge, IL 60028
847-296-7043
aeb@aeb.org

American Heart Association, National Center
7272 Greenville Avenue
Dallas, TX 75231
www.americanheart.org

Association for the Education of Children International
17904 Georgia Avenue, Suite 215
Olney, MD 20832
800-423-3563
aceihq@aol.com

Asthma and Allergy Foundation of America (AAFA)
1233 20th Street, Suite 402
Washington, DC 20036
800-727-8462
info@aafa.org

Center for Science in the Public Interest
1875 Connecticut Avenue, NW, Suite 300
Washington, DC 20009
202-332-9110
cspi@cspinet.org

Food and Nutrition Information Center (FNIC)
USDA/Agricultural Research Service
National Agricultural Library, Room 304
10301 Baltimore Avenue
Beltsville, MD 20705-2351
301-504-5719
www.nal.usda.gov/fnic

Juvenile Diabetes Foundation International
120 Wall Street
New York, NY 10005
Info@jdf.org

National Association for the Education of Young Children
1509 16th Street, NW
Washington, DC 20036
800-424-2460
www.naeyc@naeyc.org

National Dairy Council
10255 West Higgins, Suite 900
Rosemont, IL 60018
800-426-8271
www.nationaldairycouncil.org

National Meat Association
1970 Broadway, Suite 825
Oakland, CA 94612
510-763-1533

National Nutritional Foods Association
3931 MacArthur Blvd., Suite 101
Newport Beach, CA 92660
949-622-6272

Nursing Mothers Counsel, Inc.
PO Box 50063
Palo Alto, CA 94303
650-599-3669

United Fresh Fruit and Vegetable Association
727 N. Washington St.
Alexandria, VA 22314
United@uffva.org

Y

Yams, 121
Yeast, 41, 57, 75, 121
       extracts, 129
Yogurt, 51, 68, 70, 73-74, 82, 118-119, 125-
   127, 131, 133, 135, 141, 144, 156-158, 161,
   174, 176
Young children
       calcium sources, 127
       daily minimum servings, 127, 156
       iron sources, 127
       nutritional needs, 115, 126-128
       protein sources, 127
       sample menu, 128, 156

Z

Zinc, 120, 123
Zucchini, 64, 68, 111
       cake, 134
       steamed, 37
Zuppa a due colori, 136

Early Learning Environments That Work

Rebecca Isbell and Betty Exelby

The classroom environment is a vital part of a child's learning experience. ***Early Learning Environments that Work*** explores how you can manipulate furniture, color, materials, storage, lighting, and more to encourage learning through classroom arrangement. Each chapter gives you detailed illustrations and photographs to help you set up or arrange what you already have in the classroom. 192 pages.

ISBN 0-87659-256-6 / Gryphon House / 14387 / $24.95

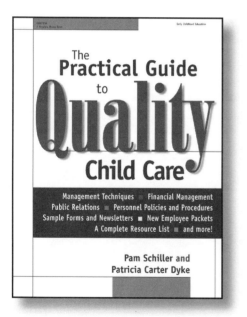

The Practical Guide to Quality Child Care

Pam Schiller and Patricia Carter Dyke

This uniquely comprehensive manual is a clear, easy-to-read handbook that provides specific guidelines for virtually every aspect of early childhood administration. Contents include: sample criteria, procedures for program development, schedules, applications, and evaluation forms. An invaluable tool for every child care facility manager. 128 pages.

ISBN 0-87659-262-0 / Gryphon House / 17356 / $24.95

Available at your favorite bookstore, school supply store, or order from Gryphon House at 800.638.0928 or www.gryphonhouse.com

Early Childhood Workshops That Work!
The Essential Guide to Successful Training and Workshops
Nancy P. Alexander

Make in-service training and workshops effective, interactive, and rewarding experiences! An effective early childhood workshop or in-service training session doesn't just happen. Good training results from the instructor's skill, knowledge, and ability to plan a session based on what participants need and want.

Early Childhood Workshops That Work! is a comprehensive guide that illustrates how to design, organize, conduct, and evaluate effective early childhood workshop and training seminars. It also includes sections on troubleshooting problem situations and designing learning materials. The author offers tips, guidance, and inside information from her years of experience as a successful workshop leader. 192 pages. 2000.

ISBN 0-87659-215-9 / Gryphon House / 13876 / $29.95

The Portfolio Book
A Step-by-Step Guide for Teachers
Elizabeth F. Shores and Cathy Grace

The Portfolio Book introduces a method to help early childhood teachers improve the responsiveness of their teaching. The ten-step guide lets teachers begin to work with portfolio assessment at a comfortable pace. This book breaks the portfolio assessment process into small, easy-to-manage steps that can be integrated painlessly into everyday teaching. 192 pages. 1998.

ISBN 0-87659-194-2 / Gryphon House / 15468 / $19.95

Available at your favorite bookstore, school supply store, or order from Gryphon House at 800.638.0928 or www.gryphonhouse.com

7787

Do Carrots Make You See Better?